BRIAN COCKERILL

THE RESURRECTION

'THE RESURRECTION'

by Jamie Boyle

www.warcrypress.co.uk
Jamie Boyle (c)

NOTE:

The views and opinions expressed in this book are those of the interviewee, in the main Brian Cockerill of Middlesbrough, they were obtained during a recorded interview and do not necessarily reflect the opinions of the author.

'Brian Cockerill - The Resurrection' 978-1-912543-29-8

All rights reserved. No part of this publication may be reproduced or transmitted in any form or by any means, including photocopying and, without the written permission of the copyright holder, application for which should be addressed to the publisher via the dealing agent at warcypress@roobix.co.uk. Such written permission must also be obtained before any part of this publication is stored in a retrieval system of any nature. This book is sold subject to the Standard Terms and Conditions of Sale of New Books and may not be re-sold in the UK below the net price fixed by the Publisher / Agent. "Brian Cockerill - The Resurrection'. Produced by Warcry Press (part of Roobix Ltd) on behalf of Jamie & Shirley Boyle, North Yorkshire (c) 2020.

Printed and bound in Great Britain by Clays, St. Ives

Book Cover Design by Gavin Parker Art - gavinparker.uk

Find out more at facebook.com/warcrypress/

DEDICATION

I dedicate this book to my wife Emma Nixon who has really put me back on the straight and narrow, we have fallen in love again after almost thirty years on from being together for the first time.

I would also like to give a special mention to my little brother Bobby who has stood by me through thick and thin more than anyone in the world and to my American Akita Scrappy who is my best friend.

CHAPTERS

FOREWORD	1
INTRODUCTION	4
TURNING TO THE DARKSIDE	14
THE BRUTAL TRUTH	20
THE TAXMAN BOOK	33
THAT DOCUMENTARY	39
RUNNING FOR MAYOR	46
LEE DUFFY: DESTROY & DESTRUCTION	53
COCKERILL SECURITY	87
REGRETS & WHAT IF'S!	91
MELTING THE ICEMAN	98
DEEP & CONTROVERSIAL	118
JUST ANOTHER MURDER ACCUSATION	124
FRIENDS & FALLOUTS	141
THE BEGINNING OF THE END	149
I'M GOING TO MAKE YOU AN OFFER YOU CAN'T REFUSE	159

BECOMING A SOMEBODY	164
THAT 'G' WORD	180
MENTAL HEALTH & REPENT	186
RAOUL THE COWARD	195
TEESSIDE'S SEEDY WORLD	204
TRUE CRIME TODAY	216
PLEASE GOD FORGIVE ME	224
WHAT IF'S EH???	235
THE ART OF VIOLENCE	242
BAD DAYS AT THE OFFICE	253
A HAPPY ENDING & AN ANGEL SENT	259

"I am the punishment of God. If you had not committed great sins, God would not have sent a punishment like me upon you".

Genghis Khan

"That's a saying I would often tell the drug dealers when I was taxing them. I told them that if they weren't ruining society then God would not have sent me to them. I would often say similar things but that was usually my calling card because Genghis Khan was the greatest taxman of all time".

Brian Cockerill 2020

FOREWORD

The Taxman's story is unique and redemptive. Rarely, has a man who has lived his life on the violent edge been caught in a vortex of Class 'A' drugs managed to detox his habits and life as effectively as Brian. He is truly a reformed character.

More than a decade ago, we did a film on Brian and he caught me in a neck lock demonstrating how powerful he was. It was terrifying.

He was always on the precipice of violence and his heavy drug habit at the time did not help. I was worried about him, his mental health and for the wellbeing of everybody around him. He was, at the time, an unpredictable force of nature. He was a fascinating criminological study and for our purposes, of course, TV gold.

He was raw, real, on the ragged edge and fuelled with recreational drugs, he was simply hyperactive and living life to the full and then some.

Brian revealed many sides of his character in our encounter filmed over several months but naturally, his latent violence was the take-home message, as you would expect. For all that you sensed, there was a real gentleman behind the brutal man-monster of a facade.

Altogether it was a surreal experience spending time with 'The Taxman'. He was so-called because of his propensity to tax the drug dealers under the threat of fearsome retribution. We never got into specifics because undoubtedly it would have put him into legal jeopardy.

To place the story into the bizarre, at the time he was also considering running for Mayor of Teesside on a 'law and order' ticket. Brian didn't get his nomination papers in on time. What a campaign that would have been to film!

Brian did his bit for the community while in tandem terrorising and terrifying parts of it in his own version of Clint Eastwood's Josie Wales. Even when he was munching steroids and other recreational drugs you knew there was a moral compass at work and now after years of abusing his body, this Silverback, as he is aptly described in the book has found his true calling.

This calling is to ward young people from following his path. The truth is that there is only one Brian Cockerill and no one could follow him if they wanted but we get the message. As a criminologist and lecturer, I recognise that the most persuasive advocates for change with errant young offenders or those likely to offend are ex-offenders and the like.

Cockerill is a FACE – he is a legend but I am confident that his true legacy will be the hundreds of young people whose futures he will change with his new life and new crusade to offer potential offenders an alternative narrative and a persuasive one, born out of the simply remarkable, unbelievable and terrifying world of 'The Taxman'.

Donal Macintyre
Criminologist & Investigative Journalist

"Brian Cockerill in 2020 is exactly what it says on the tin, a larger than life big cuddly teddy bear, like the ones you win at the fair. However, don't let that smile fool you, because behind that smile lies a deadly man."

Jamie Boyle

INTRODUCTION

Well, where do I start with Brian the bear? A figure of evil? A caveman? A Neanderthal who's just discovered fire? A big cuddly teddy bear you've just won at the fair that you just want to squeeze and squeeze until its eyes pop out?

I'll tell you where my story begins with this colossal man! I was at a boxing show in Hartlepool around 1996, I was still a schoolboy in fact. It was at The Hartlepool Borough Hall and I was on the balcony looking down with my boxing buddies Craig Turner and Neil Fairclough who were both from The Wellington ABC, I was there with the Old Vic ABC. If me and Craig were around 16 and still at school then Neil was a good 20 or 21, old enough to be going out drinking and he knew who was who and had seen much more life than the pair of us, we were just two schoolboys watching the boxing. To cut a long story short, Neil pointed down to this rather large menacing figure and said, "See him? Well that's Dave Garside who was once an ex-heavyweight boxer but he's now a promotor and he's a serious face in the North East." As I looked down at Mr Garside he looked rather sinister and I still remember to this day that on that particular evening he had the thickest bracelet on I'd ever seen in my life.

Over the years I started competing myself as an amateur boxer and would see a lot of Mr Garside and as I write this I don't think I've ever seen him smile to this day, although I know his former promoter John Spensley very well and he describes Dave Garside as a "second son who was the greatest professional he ever trained and a true gentleman".

That day the elder Neil Fairclough would go into detail to tell me and Craig Turner about these emphatic battles which had gone down in North East folklore.

In the North, where they breed tough men, the three battles of Dave Garside and Brian Cockerill are still spoken of!

That day in 1996 I hung on to every word that Neil Fairclough told us about Garside once beating Cockerill with a body shot after he'd been raving for two days with The Sayers family in Stockton, then Brian trained liked Rocky under the guidance of some old Micky like character and got his revenge and savagely beat Dave up.

In Brian's first book, 'The Taxman' it goes into detail about how, in 1992, twelve men attacked Brian and had planned to kill him. Some of those names were well known and infamous in the North-East so I won't go into that too much plus its common knowledge who the dirty dozen were.

Well in my young schoolboy mind I don't mind admitting I was blown away at these film-like stories and that's how I first came across the infamous Brian Cockerill.

Throughout my teens people would use his name even if they had never met him. The very first time I actually saw this big half-man half-ape figure was around October 1999 and I was with my friend Max Jones. Me and Max had popped up to our mutual friend Liam Henry's for some reason or another and as soon as I saw Brian I knew it was him, nobody needed to tell me, he was sat in the corner and had jet black hair. It's not often you ever see a man as big as him unless you're watching the world's strongest man, I mean I don't swear very often but this fucker was fucking gigantic. He looked like he should have been called Jambo and live in London zoo eating bananas and bamboo shoots. I didn't say a word to this overgrown gorilla but I couldn't help but stare at him up and down for all of about the fifteen minutes I was in Liam's home in Hemlington. Jambo the silverback gorilla was just sat there in the corner with a smile on his face, I don't know why. He had a white Adidas tracksuit top on and as soon as I got out I said to my mate Max, "bloody hell did you see the size of that gold chain he had on?" Max just looked back at me with a frown and said, "never mind that, did you see the size of him?" That was my first encounter with Jambo the Silverback gorilla AKA Mr Cockerill.

My next encounter was April 2003, I know these dates because I'm very much like the Rain Man from the film with Tom Cruise and Dustin Hoffman, I just don't forget things I'm a proper weirdo's weirdo.

You may have guessed by now, as this is my 13th book that I like to read/study true crime. Very much like Sir David Attenborough studies wildlife, being a true crime writer I study psychopaths, nutters and weirdos (not that I'm saying Brian falls into any one of those categories) but I like different people. Given the choice between spending time with a millionaire or a tramp on the street, I'd go sit with the tramp.

Going back to seeing this hulk of a man in Gilzeans pub, which used to be near Middlesbrough Train Station, where funny enough, in the book Lee Duffy/Viv Graham Parallel Lives there's a picture of Brian picking monster weights up but also in the back you can see Brian's best mate Bryan Flaherty clearly. I actually think it was my old buddy Craig Turner again who said, "That's that bloke over there from the Cockerill pictures." At that time Bryan Flaherty was the head doorman in Gilzeans, so me being my nosey and inquisitive self decided to walk over to Bryan Flaherty and say, "Aren't you that bloke in the Lee Duffy/Viv Graham book?" Bryan just smiled and confirmed it was him. "What's he like this Cockerill, as a person?" I asked. Anybody who knows me will be shaking their heads because you know, Pope or tramp, Jamie Liam Boyle doesn't give a fuck and will talk to anyone bar none. Nobody's better than me and I'm better than nobody else but I do like to talk! Bryan's next response really did take me by surprise and I'll never forget it as long as I live, he said, "Why don't you go and find out for yourself because he's stood over there!" As a looked over at this crowd of people I noticed Cockerill clearly stood out from the rest. He had tracksuit bottoms on with a red T-shirt with biceps bulging like Popeye and looked supremely fit. So, me being nosey Boyley I walked over to him, bearing in mind he was at No.1 on Steve Richards Crimebizz.com website at the time, I just walked over to him and said, "Aren't you that bloke off the internet?" Brian looked at me a bit taken aback, as if to say, 'How the fuck do you know that' because the internet wasn't really the big thing it is today back in 2003. He then grabbed my right hand and shook it and ran off. Not walked off, ran off which I found completely bizarre. Was the big bad Brian Cockerill scared of little old Jamie Boyle??? Haha, of course not! The reason he ran off was his best mate Bryan Flaherty was having some trouble apparently so Mr Cockerill ran over to crack a few heads and keep the trouble causers in line. In reality, they were the only two occasions where I was anywhere near Brian.

After seeing him in 2003 I read his book by Steve Richards in 2005 and if you want my honest opinion it wasn't the best of books. I'm not into slagging other authors work but in my opinion that book was rushed, in fact 12 hours in one day rushed because Brian was a crackhead and it was the last day that Steve Richards could have done it so, in reality, it wasn't Mr Richards fault it was Brian's.

In 2006 I watched the Donal Macintyre documentary, which was a lot better than the book the year before. That documentary has been watched by over 3.3 million viewers on YouTube which is up there with anything on that social media tool. That documentary is now as iconic as the Paul Sykes At Large one which made me become an author in the first place and people still talk of Brian's documentary in Teesside today.

What I must say is this, by no means is that a true reflection on the real Brian Cockerill. For a start, Channel Five filmed for over 23 hours and narrowed it down to 50 minutes and it was the most violent and nasty 50 minutes they could find. There are clips in those 23 hours where Brian was caring for kids, but the truth of the matter is that just didn't make good television so those bits were scrapped and left on the editing floor.

I've been writing True Crime books for a number of years now such as Paul Sykes, Roy Shaw, Lee Duffy, Dominic Negus, etc etc… Do you want to know the real reason why? Because nice people's books just don't sell! People want to know what makes these bad guys tick! The most amazing and unique story about the Brian Cockerill story is he's not like Lee Duffy, Speedy, Peter Hoe or Viv Graham who are all dead and gone. The man is here (by some miracle) and is here to spread the word that anyone can turn their life around. He's here and by his own admission his past is, "a load of shit" and he fully regrets it all.

When I started writing True Crime books, I did it by starting off with Wakefield's most notorious son Paul Sykes and it went from there really. Although I was into writing other bad guys books I must have been thrown the name, "Brian Cockerill" at me a dozen or so times. The truth is that even though I only lived about 8 or 10 miles away from Big Bri I had no idea how to get in touch with him. Also, even if I did manage to get in touch with Brian I was almost sure I wasn't going to be his favourite person, especially after what his former mate Terry Dicko wrote about him in 'Laughter, Madness & Mayhem' which was mostly extremely negative comments about their past 'professional' relationship. In fact, I thought I would be a walking dead man if Brian Cockerill saw me even though I'm just the author/messenger boy if you like.

For those of you who read Terry's first book 'Laughter, Madness & Mayhem' then you'll know just how much of an asbestos tongue Terry Dicko has but the fact of the matter is it was nothing to do with me. It's actually the only book out of them all that says on the front, "As told to Jamie Boyle." Believe it or not but I actually watered down what he really wanted to put, but that's another story.

To cut a long story short Terry, in his ultimate wisdom, told me to message Brian's girlfriend at the time, which I did. Unsurprisingly I got a message back from Brian saying that he didn't want to know me and that I should stop slagging him off on YouTube. In actual fact, I've never slagged Brian off ever on YouTube but I suppose I was the guy interviewing Terry Dicko and it was him with the forked tongue so I could see his point. Brian told me he didn't want to know me ever which made me think a few things about him. One that he was an arrogant bastard and two he didn't realise the platform I could offer him. I then got a few messages from Brian's then girlfriend apologising profusely, but I told her I understood and it wasn't her fault. She told me Brian had a bee in his bonnet about me which I took as he wanted to snap me in half like a Silverback would do. So, I thanked her for the warning and I noted it down to try not to meet Big Bri down any dark alley's in the next few years unless I had a rocket launcher.

To be quite honest I was pretty gobsmacked but at least I'd reached out to him and now I knew where I stood and don't ask me why, but I knew he'd need me before I needed him again.

Around five days later I got a phone call saying, "is this Jamie Boyle because this is Brian Cockerill?" I just said "it is Jamie Boyle but this isn't Brian Cockerill" as I'd lost count of the times I'd been threatened with Brian Cockerill by trolls not to mention Freddie Flintstone to Bernie Slaven. Anyway, after speaking to this alleged "Brian Cockerill" it suddenly dawned on me that his voice identically matched his from the Donal Macintyre documentary and I thought, 'OOH SHIT'. Then I just told him, "look I'm an author and whatever Terry Dicko put in his book I was just doing my job" which he totally 100% got which really did surprise me.

After we chatted for over one hour (and believe me he can match me for talking) he agreed to come around my house to do this book, but then I started thinking it was a ploy. Maybe what he really wanted to do is to find out where I lived and kidnap me then bury me up Eston Hills. I even suggested this to Terry Dicko but he told me that wasn't Brian's style.

Brian came around my house with his little brother Bobby around 4-5 days later and he shocked me in many different ways. One he never beat me up, which was a good start, two he was far more articulate than he came across in his documentary and three what a big fucking lump he was. I don't think you really realise just how big of a unit Cockerill is until he's stood over you cuddling you. Even when he's pissing about you could sense the power from him like if he really wanted to he could rip you in half like a Silverback Gorilla.

I said in the Blood Moon, which is the second book I did on Lee Duffy, that the difference between Duffy and the average guy on the street was Duffy was an athlete. He was wiry, he was rangy like Thomas Hearns, Gerald McClellan and Deontay Wilder, they may have only been thin and stripped off but they were built like a wedge, their punches would have knocked walls down. Particularly Lee Duffy's in the last year of his life when Craig Howard had beefed him up to 17st 9lbs.

In my opinion, the difference between Brian Cockerill and the other street criminals was Cockerill was a fully-fledged athlete but in a different way. No, he couldn't have danced rings around you with speed, agility and bad intentions to really do you damage, but let him grab you in the corner and there's maybe only twelve men on the planet that would be capable of getting free from his vice like hold. He was a real-life monster with the strength of a 7ft wild bear.

I'm not in the slightest bit a violent man in life, yes I was an amateur boxer for a few years but I'm not a fighter in fact, I've winced at some of the things I've had to type in here. What is frightening is imagining the damage Cockerill could do to you if he had you for only 15-20 seconds, it doesn't even bear thinking about does it?! Whereas Duffy really wanted to hurt you badly, I believe Cockerill was a much nicer man but still cross him at your peril.

As I'm writing this the Brian Cockerill PR train is picking up. He's been on the James English, The Original African and Shaun Attwood podcasts and at the moment the skies the limit for the big fella with James English 2 all set for Spring not to mention channel 5 etc… Better late than never, but in my opinion, he should have been doing this 15 plus years ago.

If you want me to sum Brian Cockerill up for you then he's a good guy who's done a lot of very bad things. From now on though I'm sure it's going to be alright with Emma (Brian's new wife) and Shirley Whirley (Mrs Boyle) by his side so he never slips ever again. Also not forgetting I'd have to punch his head right in for wasting my time HA HA!

Big Bad Bri now has a new vocation in life and it's not taxing people it's helping people. It may have taken him two thirds of his life to wake up and smell the coffee but Brian is a man who's been there and worn the T-shirt and if it makes a difference to even one of the youth of today and they learn from Brian's mistakes it will make it all worthwhile.

God bless,

From your friend,

Jamie Liam Boyle

"A leader can never be happy until his people are happy."

Genghis Khan

CHAPTER 1

TURNING TO THE DARKSIDE

I would like to start this book off by saying that, over the last ten years, if you have ever heard any stories of my head completely falling off leading to me becoming a fully blown crackhead then it was all 100% true. I was really bad and you couldn't get any worse than what I was. Believe it or not, I had never touched a drug in my life until I was twenty-six and a half. It was around the time after Lee Duffy had been shot for the second time by the Birmingham lads in 1991 and I was using copious amounts of crack cocaine as a painkiller. Everybody knows me and Lee had our ding-dongs but after that, we ended up being the best of friends.

It was Lee who introduced me to the dark side, exactly like in Star Wars, except I was Luke Skywalker and he was Darth Vader. I remember how I ended up taking drugs for the first time, it was me and Lee, we had been out and made over £700 that day taxing drug dealers. It was Lee who said we should get a bit of coke but at that time I had never taken a drug in my life, Lee said, "trust me you'll love it Brian" so he ordered some.

There was only me, Lee and Craig Howard together. Craig was a bodybuilder and was 7th in the Mr Universe competition. At that point in my life, I was extremely green and so gullible whereas Lee, he was as streetwise as they came, Lee had been in and out of jail all of his life and I had not even been arrested yet. That day me, Lee and Craig ended up going to Gateshead for some cocaine. We ended up in someone's house, I had no idea who's house it was but Lee took me in the kitchen and gave me this line of powder and I took it, I thought it had no effect on me.

A little while later whilst we were driving back to Middlesbrough I told the pair that the stuff Lee had given to me was doing fuck all and I couldn't even feel it. Lee was drinking a tin of coke in the front but as soon as he heard what I'd just said he spurted cola from his mouth all over Craig Howard's car and the pair of them were in fits of laughter. Lee said, "Brian you've never shut up for almost two hours man." At that point, I didn't know what was about to take place and I just thought that was all you could do with cocaine, until we arrived back in Teesside.

Lee and Craig took me to this house which was owned by a female bodybuilder who was Craigs girlfriend and I can even remember the address which was on Hampden Street in Stockton. Craig told me that his girlfriend preferred it when he hung around with me instead of Lee because it scared her just to be in his company. She always said she could enjoy having the gear with me but if she had it with Lee it would scare her because he'd always be up shadow boxing or just being hyperactive.

Another thing Craig told me was that one day when I chased Lee he thought I was Viv Graham, he told Lee I looked fuck all like him and it was because he was off his head on drugs, but when you see me up close you'll see I look nothing like my Tyneside nemesis. Craig used to tell Lee that he knew who I was because he saw me competing in bodybuilding competitions. Lee used to say that I couldn't be that hard because I took my time looking for him when I had that broken finger after our fight, but Craig said, "yes maybe so Lee, but he still came and nobody else would have the balls to come looking for you."

15

Now when I was in the house, I don't know if it was the drugs or just Lee in general but I started getting a bit paranoid with him being there. Don't forget this wasn't long after the fight that we had in Redcar when he walked up to me and punched me for no reason. I started thinking that any second now Lee's going to get me completely off my rocker, like he was fattening me up for the kill, then he was going to try and take my head off again which Lee Duffy was just a master at. Then Lee asked me to stand up and show Craig and his girlfriend how good I was on the pads, by then he'd got some boxing gloves out and pads so I was convinced that Lee was about to lay me out by landing a sneaky one on me. I don't know why I got up but I had my chin glued to my shoulder, I had my hands up and I was doing whatever Lee was asking me to throw, combinations on the pads in threes and fours. At the same time, I'm thinking if Lee starts in this tiny front room he hasn't got a chance because he can't dance about and box me because I'll grab him and wrestle him through the window. At that point, I was arguably one of the strongest people in the world in 1991 and breaking records for fun so I knew he couldn't have beat me if I'd have got hold of him.

Sure enough, it was down to me just being paranoid and Lee didn't try anything but Lee was complimenting me by saying to Craig that it was beyond belief that I was as big as I am and that I was still so fast. Then Craig Howard the bodybuilder had a go with Lee on the pads and Lee was just taking the piss out of him by saying his punches were like he was trying to bench press 500lbs. Craig was slow and clumsy and didn't have a great deal of power behind his monotonous thuds.

After us three were pissing about for maybe twenty minutes on the pads Lee told Craig, "go wash the gear up". I had no idea what was even going on, that was until Craig came from the kitchen with this test tube/Bunsen burner looking thing. Then he had this plastic bottle and all the rest of the kit they needed. Well I was looking in sheer amazement thinking 'what the fucks going on here' at Lee and Craig but the pair seemed to be in their element and it appeared that they were experts in whatever they were about to do. Lee then turned to me and said, "here big man have a go of this" with a very sinister smile. Well I had a go of whatever he just offered me and after maybe ten seconds the thing blew my head off and I was high as a kite. That was my first hit and it was such an incredibly good feeling. If only I knew at that point the misery it was going to cause me for the next quarter of a century eh!

That night we did crack cocaine from 6pm to about 4am in the morning. Lee told me we'd smoked over £700 worth of crack between the three of us. When we'd finished we went to Lee's best mate Neil Booth's house. Neil was there with his girlfriend and we continued to have more crack and we continued to enjoy ourselves, that was until Lee went to the toilet and when he came back Lee noticed a huge block of crack missing from the table. "Who has touched that crack?" Lee calmly asked! Then before anyone could answer Lee softly whispered, "I know it wasn't the big fella (meaning me) and I know it's not Boothy and I also know it's not Neil's girlfriend so there's only one person it could be according to my calculations and that's you Craig." Well, you could have cut the atmosphere in the room with a knife. I myself was starting to get embarrassed and I hadn't even done anything. "You've taken that gear Craig" Lee very calmly said. "Aah howay Lee I haven't, behave I swear to god on my mam's life" Craig said. Then Lee again very politely and ultra-calmly said, "I tell you what it is Craig, if I'm wrong I'll apologise but what you're going to do now is take your clothes off so I can check." In situations like that, I would have lost my temper but Lee was very methodical and calculated like the police are or the top barristers in the High Courts. Lee again told Craig that if he was innocent he had nothing to worry about so to get stripped off. Even I told Lee to behave because he was spoiling the mood but Lee told me to trust him because he knew it was Craig who'd stolen the gear. Craig then took his shoes, trousers, top and T-shirt off then said, "see I told you I haven't taken it."

Craig Howard, by the way, was one fucking huge bloke and looked just awesome. At this point, Craig Howard must have thought he'd gotten away with it and was almost at the point of tears. Then Lee looked him right in the eyes, smiled and said, "get ya underpants off now" and with that a big block of crack fell out of the waistband of his underpants. Lee then looked at us all and just said, "TOLD YA". Craig then began saying how sorry he was but Lee chased him out of the house in disgust. When Craig had been banished we smoked all the rest of the gear and I ended up sleeping on Neil Booths front room floor but I couldn't get to sleep because I could hear Boothy at it all morning with his girlfriend and by that point the birds were chirping and it was light. Lee was on the settee. All 6ft 4 of him was across the sofa. That evening with Lee Duffy and friends was the start of my problems with drugs, I just didn't know it at the time.

"I've written a lot of true crime books such as Paul Sykes, Lee Duffy, Roy Shaw and Dominic Negus etc etc… It swings in roundabouts and in the end, well the end product is that they became what they didn't want to become and I think Brian Cockerill is just another statistic of this."

Jamie Boyle

CHAPTER 2

THE BRUTAL TRUTH

As I told you, I first took crack cocaine with Lee Duffy in 1991 but it went on for years after that. After Lee had died I started going out with a girl from Roseworth and she was into drugs and I started doing things with her but only very occasionally. I'm not blaming anyone else but myself here, I'm just explaining how I first came into that world. Me and this girlfriend would start taking speed together, then it went on to be a couple of E.

Before I was introduced to the world of drugs I was only working the doors and even then, although everyone around me was on drugs, I didn't take anything.

Another guy who also showed me that side of the drugs world was Speedy (Mark Hornsby) when I started doing bits of taxing with him.

One day me, Lee Duffy and Craig Howard went to visit Speedy at Acklington prison in Morpeth and Lee Duffy walks in the visiting room smoking a big spliff. He even had the audacity to shout at one of the screws, "ERE BOSS GIZ A LIGHT!" Then when he gave him a light he blew smoke in the screws face. I could see the other screws looking at the guy with the smoke in his face as if to say, 'please don't do anything it's Duffy'. Lee then sat for the next two hours with his feet up on the chairs and going to other people's tables, despite the fact that he wasn't supposed to talk to everyone he knew in that jail.

I'm not kidding you but everybody knew who he was in that jail that day and Lee was off his fucking Barnet.

Speedy went on to get shot and killed but we'll come to that later.

When me and Speedy were taxing we'd always end up washing a bit of cocaine and smoking it together, then of course, I'd have to take a bit home for my girlfriend and we'd end up doing it together but at that point in the early 1990s, I could take it or leave it. It hadn't really gotten hold of me like it would go on to do, so it was all fun and games and only really for recreational use. I was with that girlfriend and I was so loyal to that girl for over five years, never even looked at another girl but I started thinking I'd never really had a life. All I'd done was just train all my life from my early teens and now I was becoming a somebody around Teesside the thoughts and the temptation to do other things was well and truly to set in.

It was inevitable but me and my girlfriend split so I found myself single and going out playing the field like a lot of young lads do. Also because of this new reputation as a bad boy I was developing, plus because of my size I was getting a lot of attention from the opposite sex which I'd never really had before. From the ages of 24 to about 32 I was in my prime and I was really really big as you can see from my Facebook social media page. I mean I've always been a big guy at 6ft 3 but that was when I was at another level to even most of the contestants of the world's strongest men. Even when I went to jail and I lost a few stones I wasn't that bothered because I was still over 20st and I hadn't stopped my training. Back at that time in my life I was going out on a weekend and munching as many ecstasy tablets like the Cookie Monster with cookies and then I'd go home and be alright. Then after a couple of years the drugs got more serious. Particularly around the late 1990s my mind was just all about a bit more crack, a bit more crack then a little bit more crack.

After I finished with my girlfriend I started seeing another girl and that's when I started to really cane the stuff. Me and her were just on it every night. At that time when I was with her I was also banned out of most of the town of Middlesbrough because the police put a ban on me which saw me stay in for six months, which then led to me smoking crack in my house because I couldn't do anything else. I would say all my drug taking before 1995/96 I had a grip of but after that I was crack mad. If I wasn't smoking it I'd be thinking of making pipes in my mind or thinking about smoking myself stupid on the night. I'd be thinking of which drug dealers to tax so I could fund my newly formed habit. When I became addicted to crack cocaine I stopped the training I'd been doing all my life and the weight was falling off me. It didn't help that I was now in Elvis Tomo's company a hell of a lot and he was in the same boat as me with drugs. Even though by now I was a fully blown drug addict and half the man I once was I could fight for fun still. Me and Elvis were on drugs daily together and he'd be doing the taxing with me but he could fight for fun also being a former professional boxer so we were more than a match for the dealers of Teesside. Me and Elvis did start training together and we'd go running and lifting weights but we'd ruin all our good work during the day by smoking the crack at night. At times me, Elvis and my girlfriend at the time would have crack cocaine fuelled sessions for hours and then from about 1996 for the first time I started to become really affected with paranoia.

As I told you for the six months I was on a police curfew and under house arrest and every night maybe 2-3 times the police would drive to my house and I'd have to show my face at the window. At that time I was having a load of trouble with nightclub owners and drug dealers so the police wanted me off the scene. Sometimes I'd have just had a crackpipe and maybe 20 seconds later the police would come so I'd have to show my face at the window high as a motherfucker and they'd wave back at me and off they'd go, then come back in another few hours for the same thing to happen again. I think it all got too much for me and I'd get paranoid that they knew what I was doing and they'd then come in with the riot squad and twenty officers. I know a lot of the times I'd run upstairs and put my head under the shower so if I looked weird from the drugs I could pretend I'd just come out of the shower. I know it was silly of me but that's the way I used to think.

I know once upon a time I was a bad man, I'll admit that, but the police in those days were really out to get me for anything. Nothing is a better example than when I was sentenced to 30 months for a daft driving offence by failing to stop in 1995. Everyone else who got an offence like that would have got a slap on the wrist but because it was Brian Cockerill I got two and a half years. It was ironic because when I got to prison I met people who'd ran people over who had got lesser sentences than me.

I was released from prison in 1997 finally but before my release, I had been given a two-day weekend release from jail on home leave and I made up for the lost time by popping into Terry Dicko's place 'The Steampacket' to get off my barnet on ecstasy tablets. It was at that weekend I met Amanda who I went on to be with for over 17 years. As soon as I saw Amanda I thought she was beautiful, she reminded me of a young Melinda Messenger.

After that weekend I went back to jail to finish the rest of my sentence. Upon my release I went back to my Mam's in Hartlepool for a month then stayed at my brother Skinny's (now sadly passed) and I was just trying to settle back into society. It was in 1997 that me and Amanda became a proper couple and for a while I got away from crack cocaine but I'd only swapped from one bad thing to another because I was now really into my E tablets, getting among the drug scene and just wanted to party 24/7. I would maybe keep away from crack for maybe the best part of 6 months but now I was on the powder.

It was at the end of 1997 that I was back around Elvis Tomo's flat and back on the pipe and I was as wild as ever.

In 1998/99 yes I was bad on the drugs but at the same time I was training for the world's strongest man because I'd got an invite from them, that was until I received a leg injury. It's a shame because I was just under 24st and breaking all kinds of records in the gyms across Teesside.

Because I wasn't able to compete in the world's strongest man I began to feel sorry for myself and began to take crack again to ease the pain. Looking back with hindsight now I know it was just an excuse to go back on the drugs and from that point, within 6-7 months I went from 23st 10lbs to 17st 6lbs in the year 2000.

Sometimes what I would do was have no crack at all for 6 months and I'd think that was some kind of achievement which is just sad isn't it?! Maybe the worst of all times with me and that evil drug crack was 2010 to about 2013 which was when Amanda got up and finally left me. Amanda leaving me in 2013 saved both mine and her lives but again I'll get to that further along in the book.

Between those years of 2010 to 2013 I found several bugs in my home and car, I'm not talking about creepy crawlies either, I'm talking about police bugs, so that set my paranoia off big time.

Now, I know it was the national crime squad that had bugged me thinking I was going to be discussing murders. I knew some of the alleged offenders in a drugs bust which saw twelve big names and Middlesbrough criminals taken off the streets for 6 months in 2001 and put on remand until it all collapsed, were caught because they had bugs put in their televisions, so I started ripping my telly to pieces also. Sometimes I used to turn to Amanda when I was off my head and I'd say, "are you an undercover copper?" Then I'd persist in asking her when was it that the police turned her against me to work for them? I thought the police had got to Amanda like they do to members of the Mafia when one of them squeals and informs. Some nights I'd been hammering the crack that much it was called psychosis and it's like having a break from reality. I'd got that bad when I was on that shite that I'd look at Amanda and I'd think, that's not even our lass! Then I started thinking she was a robot and she wasn't a human. Then I started thinking it wasn't Amanda but she was a copper robot and her eyes were cameras and she was watching me so I started nipping her to see if she felt pain. When I then nipped her I can't have done it properly and it had no effect so I even thought, 'I knew it she's a fucking robot!' That was until I did it again and she yelped out loud and said, "Brian what the fuck are you doing?"

To be honest there were times when I was so off my box that I thought I was on a gameshow. I know you readers might be laughing reading this because it's all sheer insanity on top of pure madness at the highest level but that's how bad I got. The next day I would wake up and I'd feel so embarrassed because of the utter nonsense I'd come out with. Also I would shout and bawl at Amanda for nothing. She never got paranoid like me but at the end of our relationship she became as bad as me when every little noise happened.

If me and her had been to Redcar on the day and then it said something about Redcar on the telly me and her would think something was happening if we were on that devils dandruff. Basically, that evil drug would make you word associate anything and it sent you bonkers. Sometimes on the telly if a greyhound came on I'd be sitting there thinking, hang on a minute, I've just been to my mate Dicky Dido's who had a greyhound so the paranoia was unreal.

That was when I started with the sleeping tablets to bring me down which really was just another addiction. I've never taken heroin in my life but I was well into diazepam, temazepam, zopiclones etc etc... At times when I was on the crack I'd spend £150 on an 8th, £10 for the fags because you need cigarette ash for the pipe to the people who don't know and then all the paraphernalia that was needed, it all adds up. That was just an average night for me.

I'll tell you a funny but also quite tragic story. I got £1000 one night on a job which was cash in-hand. I paid £20 to the electric, £20 to the gas, £20 for groceries and I spent over £900 on crack cocaine that night. When all the crack had gone I remember clearly thinking that I'd just wasted £60 on household items! That's an awful thing to admit but if I tell you that then you'll understand just how bad I was. At times in my life I've wasted over £5,000 on crack but at the time saw it as I'd wasted £100 on shopping!

Another scary true fact I don't like thinking about was when me and Amanda did two ounces of crack in one week which is a frightening statistic because that was fifty six grams and any normal person should have been dead. That's not me bullshitting you that's the real truth.

When you tax drugs you're effectively getting them for free and you don't care. At times I was going into houses on my own across Teesside which were full of Yardies from London, Leeds, Manchester and Birmingham and I was nicking their gear and chasing them out of the crack houses. One night I took forty stones of crack and I went home and smoked the fucking lot over about five or six days. One night I went in a crack house and there was about eleven of them in there, Jamie Barker from Middlesbrough was there to witness this to anyone who thinks I'm talking shit. In fact one of the black lads in the crack house, I won't mention his name but he was a lad from Leeds and he'd appeared on Big Brother. The story was that I went into the house and I asked them to give me a bit on tic because my money went in the bank at midnight and this was just before. Of course, I was told no and that it was no money no gear. As the former Big Brother contestant told me no I noticed this huge big black man laying across the settee smiling at me with a mouthful of gold teeth. It was in the old Salvano's crack house in the town in Boro truth be told. Well I wasn't too pleased to be told no but considering who I was and what I was about I wasn't surprised that they told me I couldn't have any crack and I was going to leave it at that, that was until the big black guy with a mouthful of gold teeth got up and said to Amanda, "you've been told bitch!" Well as soon as that was said I said, "hang on a minute who you calling bitch?" Then I couldn't help myself so it was 'BOOM' and you know when you've hit someone and you know you've totally fucked them, well his jaw went fishing then he hit the wall. As soon as he hit the wall another Yardie came running towards me but I grabbed him and I flung him through the front room fucking window, then another one came and I grabbed him and I tried to smash his fucking head through the telly but it wouldn't smash. To put it, in a nutshell, the whole house had erupted into sheer violence of the highest order and one of the Yardies sneaked up behind me and snapped a wooden floorboard right across my head but I didn't flinch, all I did was turn around and say, "right you want to play fucking games do you?" Then I started swinging about four of them around the front room. It was like a scene from The Incredible Hulk movie and I was going full madman like the old WWF wrestler The Ultimate Warrior and all the drug dealers just ran out of the house to the point where I had the full house to myself but I was still raging. I was gutted that there was no more lads to swing about so what I did was went through all the dealers jackets and stole all the car keys until I noticed a few of the other dealers who hadn't been involved so I left them alone. Saying that, when I saw them looking through the stair railings I just shouted at them like an angry parent at his 5-year-old kid who wouldn't go to bed, "GET TO BED YOUS AND STAY UP THERE" then I continued to ravage the house looking for whatever I could tax. All I could find was a couple of hundred quid's worth of gear but what was more valuable to me now was that I had all the dealers car keys which came in handy for my new plan that I was about to put into play. I rang the Yardi's and I told them that they could have their car keys back but that I wanted some gear which they agreed on. The deal was that they wouldn't deal with me again even though there were five of them with baseball bats. So, they told Amanda to go meet them but only in a place which was full of cameras in case I jumped out and got them all. To cut a long story short Amanda didn't give a fuck and she went to meet them, they got their keys back and we got a load of free gear so it was a good day at the office and a great night out which left a lot of drug dealers with injuries.

Another similar story like that was when I got nine ounces. Nine times out of ten every time when I taxed someone it was for crack cocaine. It wasn't because I was greedy and I was going to flood the streets of Middlesbrough with heroin. The cold reality of it was that I was ill, I was a greedy drug addict and truth be told the only bad I was doing to people was to the lowest of the low who ruin society and have never done a day's work in their lives. I wouldn't fucking dream of doing anything to proper decent law-abiding citizens, perish the thought!

The times when I was out taxing drug dealers I did a lot of good at the same time but that never got spoken of in Teesside. Stuff like getting people's stolen belongings back when they couldn't do it themselves and I didn't ask for a penny.

Also, as bad as I was on the drugs, I wasn't always on it. Sometimes I'd be clean for maybe three months by going abroad. Then there were the very bad times which were just before Amanda left me in 2013.

Looking back it must have been the Christmas in 2012 when every penny between us was going on the crack. I was selling tv's, cars, motorbikes and caravans for drugs. At one point I had about £100,000 worth of vehicles in my front garden and it all went by the wayside so much so that it got to the point that I was left driving an old banger worth £300. Even Amanda fell to bits by going from 9st to less than 7st. In the end Amanda's head looked like a lightbulb because of how frail her body had got it was terrible.

What I'd like to say is Amanda wasn't as bad as me, if you asked her and if anyone asked me I wasn't as bad as her on drugs when the harsh reality is we were both as bad as each other. We were both in this sinking ship going down and we couldn't get off it. At times we'd go to Amanda's Mam's who was a lovely woman. The family were all fantastic who were based in Thornaby. Anyway, we'd often go to Amanda's Mam's and they knew we were on shit together because they'd seen me when I was fucking huge, they weren't stupid.

Me and Amanda would tell them some ridiculous lies like we needed £100 for the car insurance which was shameful of us. I also used to tell my little brother Bobby lies like I was getting my house repossessed unless he lent me £300 and he would give me it. Bobby wasn't daft also and he could see right through me like a sheet of glass. My other siblings Jamie and Catherine also heard some belters and I got thousands of pounds off them. I truly let them down and myself down and society in general.

A lot of the youth in Middlesbrough looked at me like some kind of role model because of who I'd been but the truth was I was a pathetic crackhead who you couldn't trust. I was as rock bottom as you could possibly have got without being a rapist or a paedophile. The reason I'm revealing this to the world for the first time is because I am seeking absolution and also for the people that say, "ooh that daft Brian Cockerill's just a fucking daft crackhead", I'm admitting it now so that can't be used against me again. I know what I was more than anyone trust me.

When my brother Peter (skinny) died in 2006 I would escape to crack night and day. Peter died when I was actually filming the Donal Macintyre documentary and when I got the phone call to tell me he'd died I was on the crack. Then when I'd just heard the news I was having pipes like minutes after it because I thought it was an escape route.

"Brian Cockerill is a mountain of a man who has lived his life to the full. Like many of us, he has experienced a lot of highs and lows but has come through his life experiences with a great story to tell which he can now pass on as a guiding light. Underestimate his inner strength at your peril."

Steve Wraith Actor/Author/Promotor

CHAPTER 3

THE TAXMAN BOOK

The idea for my first autobiography, which was written by Steve Richards, came from me being involved in Julian Davies' book 'Streetfighter' in 2000.

Julian was going around Britain and speaking to all the best fighters and when he went to see my good friend Richy Horsley from Hartlepool he suggested to Steve that he speak with Brian Cockerill because I was phenomenal. When Julian came to interview me I'd been on the crack that day as well as god knows how many ecstasy tablets. Sometimes during the day I'd have E's and close the curtains, put the music on and party on my own.

Anyway going back to when Julian came before he interviewed me he asked me to go on the pads with him in my gym at the back of my house. At that point, I hadn't done any boxing for maybe four or five years as well as being a bit wrecked. Amanda was looking after us, that's one thing Amanda was brilliant at was always catering for any guests we ever had. Even though I was absolutely fucked from the drugs, Julian told me I was incredible on the pads in his broad Welsh accent.

That day Julian interviewed me for the book 'Streetfighters' and he was supposed to write 'The Taxman' but for some reason, he seemed to lose interest because he never made much money from his book 'Streetfighters.' When Julian did the PR with the newspapers he told them, "I've interviewed hundreds of fighters, but there's only one Brian Cockerill in Britain." He also told the papers that once in only a lifetime a fighter like Brian Cockerill comes around. Obviously, word must have got back to Steve Richards who was the main man in that genre (before Jamie Boyle came along obviously) that I wanted my autobiography written so he got in touch. Before we did 'The Taxman' Steve asked me to be in a book which was the third and final book which came out in 2001 on Viv Graham but it had quite a lot in about my old pal Lee Duffy. Steve Richards also told me that he was planning on doing a possible film about the life and times of Tyneside's Viv Graham and Middlesbrough's Lee Duffy but people asked him to speak with me. Steve told me that often people used to tell him that if you want to really speak with the best fighter in the North East then forget Graham and Duffy and go speak with Cockerill. Steve told me that this Cockerill name kept coming up so he just had to come and meet me and the rest is history so we did the books. Steve Richards did a chapter on me for Viv Graham's 'Final Chapter' book then he asked me to do Charlie Bronson's Solitary Fitness which was just a load of pictures of me doing these exercises in shorts. Even though I was on the crack then, I was in deep training for it and I spent a fortune on steroids to get in shape for the book although I didn't get £1 from it. I must have been mad mustn't I, but I didn't know any different.

Steve Richards then did Richy Horsley's 'On the Chin'. I know Steve Richards has taken his fair share of stick over the years but I only found him to be a lovely man, although I found his book writing methods quite bizarre. I mean for The Taxman he recorded me for twelve hours in one day but for this book, I've done it over four days. Saying that it was 100% my fault because I let him down several times saying I would meet him but because of my drug taking, I wouldn't turn up.

A lot of the times I'd be really embarrassed and I'd think I can't let him see the state I was in but I think deep down he knew what I was up to but he never said anything.

I would always come out with all kinds of crap to people like I've got this chest infection or I've got this flu when the only flu I had was Columbian flu. That first book was a huge success and I did three book signings in Book World in The Hill Street Centre, Middlesbrough and from that alone we sold 2,800 books. At that time that book outsold Jodie Marsh's and Jordan's the glamour models. People came to see me from Germany, Holland, Australia and America. It was surreal to think that these people even knew who I was. Yes, I've always been extremely well known in the Teesside area and appeared in other books but when my book came out it made me a fully blown celebrity overnight it was mental.

I think a lot of the interest that there was for that book was because there had never been a taxman before, apart from the chancellor of the exchequer.

If you want a window into what I've done then you'd have to think back to a warlord like Genghis Khan who was the best ever.

What was different about me was that people saw that everything I ever did I did with my own hands. I never used guns, knives or metal bars. I know this sounds totally narcissistic and that I'm full of shit, but I've been in houses on my own with six or seven lads and knocked them all out.

It wasn't all positives though and I was met with some sections of negativity. Some said I was just a big-headed prick but it wasn't me being that way, I was just telling the truth. If Mike Tyson told people he knocked people out then they would believe he knocked them out because he was on the tv but because I did it people said I was lying.

The people of Teesside that were in my old world knew it was the truth but the trolls on the internet in Surrey would just write a load of abuse to me online.

If you ask me if I was happy with the book then to be truthful I never had it checked out before it went to print but that wasn't anyone's fault but my own. Steve Richards gave me the script and told me to double check the stories for inaccuracies but I had better things to do like take drugs, or so I thought at the time.

The things in the book where It said I had a fight with Eddy Ellwood was wrong. What I really said was that I had a fight with someone the size of the weightlifter Eddy Ellwood. Another bit of information in the book that says I was benching 600lbs with ten reps, I didn't say that. What I really said was that I did it for three reps, but as I've said I've only got myself to blame and that wasn't Steve Richards' fault. There was also little exaggerations like when he said I was 6ft 4 but I'm 6ft 3. I think a lot of the reason why it took me over ten years to read the book myself was that I was scared of what I was going to find out.

That book has made me famous all over the world. People have known me in South America where people have shouted, "BIG BRI BIG BRI" as soon as they've seen me and asked for photographs. Even if people didn't know me they've asked me for photographs from all parts of the world when I've been fucking huge. Especially when you go to places like Greece, they really appreciate the gods

Hercules and Zeus and they really admire the hard work you've put in. I said the same thing on Donal Macintyre's documentary. When I'm in Britain people say I'm only big because I was on steroids but over in Greece they don't say things like that.

At times when I was abroad, I've curled 63KG dumbbells when most people in the gym couldn't even pick them off the floor. I've squatted 365KG which is 803LBS. I'm aware that in the first book I came across as arrogant but please, believe me, I'm really not like that and the main reason for doing this book was to have a platform once again so I can put that right.

For all the twenty to thirty hours of shooting on Macintyre, they only showed less than one hour of it and they wanted to portray me in that light, the same light the Steve Richards' book cast on me. 'The Taxman' book was done but it wasn't done the way I wanted it, whereas this one I've had a say over every single sentence and I'm only glad to have been given the chance to say what I want to say.

"I've known Brian over 25 years and heard he went through a lot of bad shit with crack addiction. I haven't seen him for years but I'm really glad he's got himself clean and doing lots of positive things by helping others Good luck mate."

Richy Horsley

CHAPTER 4

THAT DOCUMENTARY

How the Donal Macintyre documentary came about in 2006 was from another guy who wanted to put his angle on it and not Donal.

I was contacted by a man named Darren who was a lovely lad and his wife Karen who worked for the BBC and she was a producer for EastEnders. Out of the two, I got on really well with Darren but I found Karen extremely posh and almost toffee nosed. Anyway, Karen was the genius with the camera and it was Darren who was wanting to get into filming documentaries so the plan was that these two were going to film my documentary but it didn't work out as we'd planned. It's a shame that they didn't end up doing the documentary because Darren and Karen filmed me a hell of a lot in places such as pubs in Yarm and they had hours of me talking in general. At times when I was out filming with the two of them, there were people coming up to me and asking for photos and autographs, even the footballer Stewy Downing was one who came up to me for a chat. It was at the time when Stewy was flying, playing for England and he even said to my brother Bobby that he couldn't get anywhere near me because of the crowds which were constantly around me.

The reason that Darren and Karen didn't end up doing the documentary was maybe down to a slight fall out between the three of us. When they came up to speak with me the pair were staying at a hotel in Eaglescliffe but I could sense there was something not quite right. See, I'm very sharp me so when I was alone with Darren I told him that I knew there wasn't something quite right and he agreed. It turned out the pair had been arguing when I wasn't there and I knew right away that Karen didn't like me but Darren did. When Karen was asking me questions I could tell she was insinuating I was a liar even though I'd answered all her questions. I came to the conclusion that actually I didn't really care for her or her attitude, so now we were in an awkward situation.

One of the things she asked me was, "Why would the people of Teesside come to you Brian when they could just call the police?" My answer to that was that if you live on a council estate and you call the police you open the barriers to your house and car being smashed to bits but she didn't understand because she'd been born with a silver spoon in her mouth in my opinion. I was trying to be as polite as possible in explaining this and I wasn't being obtuse but it just didn't seem to register with her. What normally happens in situations like that is if there are two parties having issues then whichever one goes to the police would then be branded as grasses by the whole estate and then that's them fucked, obviously that doesn't extend to women who call the police if they're being threatened, but I was explaining that if they came to Brian Cockerill it could be resolved amicably but I knew this wasn't sinking in with Karen and I could feel her distain for me the more I was in her company.

What really sealed our fate in regards to working together was when Karen went to the toilet and I was talking, but I forgot I still had the mics on, so when I sat there saying that she was a fucking arsehole and that she was doing my head in I didn't know she was listening to everything I was saying. I wasn't being nasty about her but she heard me when I said that she was from a nice area like the Thames and here she was coming up to my manor of Teesside quizzing me but talking to me like I was fucking lying. Well it was slightly awkward when her husband Darren told me, "she's just heard every word you said Brian" so she put her foot down like a little kid and said she'd have nothing more to do with me but Darren wanted to still do it. I told Darren I wasn't being funny but he had his work cut out for himself being with her and he actually agreed with me. Darren told me that she wore the trousers in their relationship. I liked Darren and I told him that to be in a successful relationship that she needed to learn to be in a 50/50 relationship and I left it at that out of respect for Darren. We managed to put our little problem to one side and we did another 120 minutes of filming and he put it forward to the BBC but they wouldn't move forward with it because it was too violent. Whether Karen put paid to that I don't know. After I got knocked back from the BBC it was Darren who suggested we speak to Donal Macintyre and the rest is history.

Before I did The Taxman documentary I was approached by another television company who were filming Britain's Toughest Towns and it was me who took them to Skinningrove. As soon as I took them to Skinningrove the company told me in their exact words, "this is fucking perfect it's like still living in the 1970s" and they actually filmed it. One of the other things I was asked was to narrate it because of my local Middlesbrough accent but of course, Brian knew better and fucked it all up by going missing on the crack binges. I could kick myself looking back because that series was really successful and the company kept phoning me and phoning me pleading with me that they needed me to do it, but it fell on deaf ears.

Going back to the Macintyre documentary I got a call again from Darren and he said he wanted to come up with a fella named Dave Malone who was a producer. I know a lot of people who have watched my documentary think I was walking around with Donal Macintyre for the best part of three months but to be truthful Donal only came for two days and I was with Dave Malone's film crew for the rest. My one-hour documentary took in total twenty-three hours of filming then it was all narrowed down to just one hour.

I met Donal at Darlington Train Station and he explained to me just what was in store and how things worked when filming a documentary and it was made by Dare Films. I signed the contract there and then but what was sad about it was I didn't realise about the royalties, percentages, books and rights like I do now Jamie Boyle has explained them to me. Back then I was just grateful that I was having a documentary made about me and I was going to be on the telly but the reality was that people made thousands of pounds from my name. Then it was me who had the trolls saying nasty things about me on YouTube or other social media platforms. It was the same with the Steve Richards books because I only received a pittance and from only one book I might add.

If you want my view on 'The Taxman' documentary then a lot of it was funny but it focused on glamourising me taxing people and the bad things. Yes, I've been arrested for murders but I haven't committed one but the documentary wasn't interested in that side. It didn't really want to show that the seven murders I've been arrested for were mainly because the guilty parties have been using my name and I didn't in fact even know the murderers. I think to be truthful if you watch that documentary I come across as being very arrogant which really isn't me. My answer to that though was that when you're a fighter you have to come across supremely 100% confident at all times. You never saw Mike Tyson going to the ring saying, "ooh I might win and I hope I win" etc etc blah blah… I knew that a lot of my rivals across Teesside would watch that and I had to put a persona on for the cameras, but at the same time I wasn't bothered about any man in the world wanting a fight with me and that's the truth.

I was brought up with a mentality from my Mam to fight anyone and if I lost then to still get stuck in. My Mam used to say, "Brian, even if you lose then if you can put a mark on them then they'll think twice about coming back for you."

That man who was filmed in that documentary is long gone now can I please clarify that?! Yes, I Brian Cockerill can still fight but I want to be able to speak rather than lower myself and people think of me as some thug when I'm not. I have a brain quicker than most people's.

Today we're in the 21st century and if you put yourself in the public spotlight then you've got to be prepared to be shot down. Yes, I had anonymous trolls saying they were going to come and kill my wife, cut my son's head off and burn my house down etc etc… In those days I would scream, "I'LL FUCKING KILL YOU COME AND MEET ME" blah blah blah when in reality I was arguing with some 16-year-old kid who lives in Canada. One day I did get my mate who was ex SAS to track this troll down who'd said he was going to do all sorts to me and I got him on his front doorstep and strangled him and the guy pissed himself. These days I don't give a fuck about what anybody says about me because that's their opinion. I now know you can't stop what people's brains are thinking and who would want to?!

Lee Duffy (God rest his soul) used to say to me often, "Brian when the bad people say bad things about you don't worry about it, it's when the good people are saying bad things about you that you've got to worry about it" and those words that Lee said have always stayed with me.

Believe it or not but Lee Duffy was quite a sensitive soul and that man taught me a lot. Lee was really clever and streets ahead of me in psychology. Lee used to come out with all sorts and I'd think he's fucking crackers but he was always always right. When me and him would turn up at drug dealers doors and they said they'd got nothing I'd believe them, whereas Lee would know different without even using violence. I was young and green whereas Lee was an evil genius. It just shows that the point I'm trying to make is that when he hit me, I was just trying to be his friend and the only thing he had on his mind was banging this big fucker out cold to enhance his reputation which nearly worked. If Lee Duffy saw anyone big he wanted to put them to kip so he could prove that he was the best. All Lee wanted was to come from a nobody who had been bullied to a somebody and he was like that for all of his short adult life. He may have only been here a short while but boy did that man leave a legacy.

What I'd like to finally let people know and I've never revealed this before, although I never received a penny for that documentary, I told the makers of that film to give it to Lee Duffy's daughter in her aid to go and swim with dolphins after the poor girl had her eye shot out by another kid with a pellet gun. I wanted to do something for my big pal who isn't here today.

"A lot has been said over the last three decades. Lee Duffy pulverised Brian Cockerill, Brian Cockerill was just far too much for any man with that vice-like grip. One thing is for sure, Brian did well to even get back up on his feet because Lee Duffy's punches would have knocked walls down. In a power and fighting sense, the Duff was a bad bad man."

Jamie Boyle

CHAPTER 5

RUNNING FOR MAYOR

After the explosion of the documentary, a lot of people started saying to me on a daily basis that I should be the Mayor of Middlesbrough. I never really seriously considered it until it dawned on me about Ray Mallon. One day I just thought, hang on a minute he's been kicked out the police force and it was alleged it was due to being linked with shady corruption. Technically, he's possibly more of a villain than I am because all I've got on my police records are driving bans.

Mr Mallon was investigated for over four years and it cost the taxpayers over four million and then it got swept under the carpet and flung out of courts. Then, in the end, as reported in the Evening Gazette in February 2002, he pleaded guilty to all disciplinary charges against him regarding the controversial Operation Lancet inquiry. Even a well-known famous MP has gone on record to say, "Mr Mallon was linked to a trail of corruption."

I think I only had to look at the Ray Mallon fiasco and the fact that eventually, he became the Mayor of Middlesbrough and that gave me the bottle to try myself if you like. If you asked me my opinion on why Mr Mallon got off with what it was alleged he had done, I would have said he had too much on the whole force in general. I think it was a case of, if I go down I'm taking the whole lot of you down with me and that's why it got swept under the carpet the way it did, but like I said, that's just my opinion.

I suppose with me being who I was and having the name I did in Teesside with people coming to me day and night I started thinking, I could be the fucking Mayor myself!!! It was only what I'd been doing anyway, helping people on a daily basis so that's really where it all started for me.

After putting the idea to a few close friends of mine, it was met with their full backing so I started going around a few of the local council estates. On Macintyre's documentary, you can see me walking around Grove Hill. When I was on the Grove Hill estate I helped one woman who was a nurse and she'd had problems with some of her neighbours who were smackheads and they'd been leaving needles all over the place. It was because of this that it was stopping her seeing her daughter and when she wanted access she had to see her daughter at her mother's because these low lives were making it impossible. Another neighbour close by to this nurse was a bag of nerves because of them and directly over the road was another set of neighbours who couldn't sell the house because of these rats. Now, these three sets of neighbours had reported these rats to the council several times but nothing was getting done so, in my opinion, it was up to me to sort it which I did. As I was about to give these smackheads a knock a police car flew around the corner and shouted, "what's happening here then Brian?" When I told them what was about to go down the officer winked at me and said, "we haven't been" and then drove off. Well I walked towards the front door and I booted the front door but nothing happened then I started thinking, I must be losing my touch and my key doesn't work as well as it used to. Anyway I eventually worked out that these rats had put a settee up against the door so it didn't matter if it was fucking King-Kong and not Brian Cockerill nobody was getting through that. What they'd done was put the settee between the stairs and the door but after about twenty minutes of kicking it, I finally got it open and about twenty of the walking dead like Vampires seeing sunlight finally ran out and ran to safety.

Now I had every smackheads hideout in Grove Hill closed down I put a few of my Cockerill Security signs on the house if any of the living dead tried to come back. You know what the best thing of the whole story is after I sorted it I went back around that area exactly 12 months later and the nurse now had her little girl living with her, the couple over the road had sold the house and the old dear bad with her nerves looked like a new person. When I walked up the streets and they saw me some of them were shouting, "here's our hero." An elderly man from that street told me how they could only thank me from the bottom of their hearts but I didn't want any payment. Seeing the difference I had made was good enough.

Another similar story was when my friend Liam Henry got a call and asked me to go down. Apparently, some relations of Liam's were being tortured by a gang of kids. What these kids were doing was shining them red laser pens in their windows at all times in the morning. The occupants were kicking on for 90 and had lived through the second world war for these little bastards to torture them for the sheer entertainment of it, well not on my watch. I eventually went to the door of who was responsible and they wouldn't answer, so I used my key (size 12s) and it came off its hinges but as soon as I've done that the guilty parties have ran out the back and fucked off. Sometimes I did that and let them get away because I knew that was going to be enough to deliver a warning and whatever was going on stopped that very second. I knew these people would be running off thinking, fucking hell I could have been killed there if Big Bri got me." To be truthful as much as them kids deserved throttling and talking some sense into I didn't really want to hurt these kids. People will always be scared by the thought of violence much greater than the act of violence itself and I learned that a long time ago. It's the psychology of it that hits home hard.

When I sorted that problem out with the laser pen gang I turned around and all the neighbours were out trying to offer me over £100 but I told them I didn't want a penny, I did it to help. A young lass with a baby in a pram came over and cuddled me saying how she couldn't sleep because of what this gang were doing to her and everyone on the street. I returned to the street later and this old lady ran out and shouted, "OI BIG FELLA I've made you this apple pie." It makes me well up today when I look back and reflect on some of the things I've done like that which, unless you know Brian Cockerill, it doesn't get spoken about. I've been to jobs when I've ended up giving old fella's £20 notes but that never gets spoken of because people only want to talk about Brian Cockerill the fighter or the crackhead.

On another job, I was paid to evict some squatters and when I've arrived, unbeknown to me a woman opened the door and she had a family of children in there. Well, straight away I couldn't do it because I had a bad life growing up with my family. Anyway, when I was in this poor family's home I noticed mould all over the walls and these kids are sat there freezing I ended up giving the family money. Then I went back to the guy who'd hired me and I told him if you think I'm putting them five kids and their Mam on the streets then you can stick your fucking job up your arse. This guy must have owned maybe two hundred houses and when he told me that they were only scum I told him he was a horrible horrible man and I put the phone down. At home, I had two electric radiators in my caravan. I eventually sold that caravan for crack but in there I had two radiators and I went back to that house and I gave them the two heaters for those young kids, I bought the kids some boxes of chocolate and give the mam £50 and told her to get some food in for the kids. Ironically I was sent there to make money but it ended up costing me money but I couldn't have done it any other way. It makes me shed a tear now when the kids, who had nothing, were shouting up at me, "thank you Mr."

A job I did which wasn't debt recovery but the taxing of ten grand was when I went to the house with a mate but left empty handed and gave the kids inside a tenner each. There's some things on this earth you just can't do, especially when kids are involved. I couldn't have fucking thrown that poor woman on the street with her five kids for all the money in the world. I did a lot of jobs like that but bad people were involved and I always got them out the same day.

It was due to doing deeds like that which got people pleading with me to run for Mayor so that's where the idea came from in the first place. I even had community wardens telling me that they were going to vote for me and I had more or less the full backing of the whole of Middlesbrough but in truth I didn't even run for it because I ended up back on the crack.

All the good work I laid down I ruined it all by taking drugs. I joke about a lot of things in life but can you imagine if I had made it to become the Mayor of Middlesbrough? I'd have probably fucking sold the gold chain for crack! I'd have probably taken the Mayor's chain to Ramsden's and I'd have got a fortune for crack on that chain if I pawned it.

No, jokes aside, it was around that time I pawned my own gold which was over thirty grands worth for only three grand so maybe it was a blessing I never became the Mayor in the end eh. I know I never ran for Mayor in the end but to be honest I was gaining the trust of the thousands in Middlesbrough such as schoolteachers, bankers and political figures it was unbelievable. Real law-abiding citizens were backing me and I can only apologise for letting you all down for not going through with it. Even today in 2020 I get many many people in Asda, Tesco or Morrisons just wanting to shake my hand telling me that they wanted to thank me for doing this that and the other good deeds and sadly, half the time, I can't even remember doing them.

"When you eliminate the impossible, whatever remains however improbable must be the truth."

Arthur Conan Doyle

CHAPTER 6

LEE DUFFY: DESTROY & DESTRUCTION

The very first time I heard the name Lee Duffy was around the late 1980s when I was working the doors for John Black. If ever he was out of prison then the whole of Teesside would talk of this young kid and what he got up to. Then when he was in prison Middlesbrough would just go that bit quieter because Lee was up to everything when he was out.

One of the first things I heard of Lee was when he hit a lad in Redcar called Bernie McDevitt about 1987. Lee received a large sum of money to go and break Bernie's jaw. Bernie was a big lad himself but Lee walked into a pub in Redcar on his own and walloped him. In the end Lee was arrested but he had to get John Black to have a word with Bernie to drop the charges. In reality, I don't think that even Lee Duffy wanted to be a drug dealer, but he just didn't want to pay for them either. How he got his job in the first place in Rumours was that one of the bouncers said to him, "if you can beat him up (another bouncer) you can have a job here which is exactly what he did.

The Lee I knew definitely based himself on Kevin Duckling. Lee used to have the same hair as Ducko and even the same tache.

The last time Lee got out of prison was May 1990 and I always remember John Black telling me that this Lee Duffy was about to get out soon and just how much I'd like him when I met him. John Black told me he was very much cut from the same cloth as me, could fight for fun and wasn't scared of anyone. John said that when Lee was back in society he would make sure that he'd introduce us.

The day I would meet Lee Duffy for the first time is one I'll never forget and is now embedded in Teesside folklore. I was with a lad named Kevin Kilty and we'd been to visit a lad in prison when we saw Lee Duffy and his mate Faily. Me and Kevin had just come out of a Greek restaurant called El Greko's not far from Redcar High Street. How me and Lee came about meeting was he was going to score a bit of smoke and I was going to the same place only for different reasons. So, that brought us into close proximity. Although I don't think Lee Duffy smoked cigarettes, he would smoke joint after joint like people would smoke fags and Neil Booth would confirm this.

When I became friends with Lee he would be permanently stoned that was his thing. I think being completely wired was just Lee's normal thing and if you can remember Jimmy Saville saying, "NOW THEN NOW THEN" that's exactly what he used to say. Another thing Lee was always shouting was, "OI OI" and he'd often put them both together so they were Lee's trademark sayings. Lee copied saying "now then now then" from Craig Howard as that's what he always used to say first.

Going back to my first meeting with Lee Duffy, he didn't have any idea I was Brian Cockerill and I didn't know he was this Lee Duffy I'd heard so much about. I don't think we'd have even come to each other's attention until Faily said to Lee, "look at the size of that big fucker Lee I bet you can't fight him?" Afterward Faily told me that Lee's reaction to him was, "wanna bet? I bet ya I can!" At the time

Lee Duffy was 25 so that would have made me 26 but I was green as grass compared to him. Lee had been in and out of jail all his life and I don't think I'd even been caught jaywalking across the road. At that time all Brian Cockerill was about was going to the gym, I didn't know anything about being a gangster like Lee Duffy did or taxing drug dealers etc...

On that day me and Lee had that fight I would say I was at my peak and was touching almost 24st and at my strongest ever there's no doubt about it. I was a monster in appearance and that's what Lee saw in me so he could make his fearsome rep even bigger. There's been a lot of rubbish spoken of what really happened between me and Lee Duffy but I'll tell you exactly what happened once and for all to clarify any doubt. When Lee and John came up to talk to me I thought he was going to say, "oh I'm Lee Duffy, John Black's told me all about you" but he had other ideas. At the time I had my finger in a splint so my right hand was completely useless. As I was talking to the pair I noticed that Faily had a bottle of Holsten Pils in his hand. As I was stood with the pair it was Kevin Kilty who told me it was Lee Duffy and that we should beat it sharpish because obviously, Kevin knew all about Lee whereas I was green. That was the difference I think with Lee because at that time I just wanted to be his friend. I think it was Kevin who told us again that we should go, so as we went to walk away Duffy shouted, "OI OI" and waved us back over so we walked back over and I stood right in front of him square on and thick as shit. It didn't occur to me at all what was about to take place in the shape of a left hook from The Duffer which was like being hit by a train by the way! As I was stood in front of the Duffer I was about to shake his hand and say, "my names Brian, John Black has told me all about you" when all of a sudden I felt 'BOOM' and felt an almighty thud like I'd never felt in my life. I'm not kidding you I saw more stars than Patrick Moore. The fact is that Lee walloped me that day for no reason at all other than because of my size and he was being egged on by his mate. I did hit the deck with my arse after Lee smacked me but I was so enraged that I instantly flew back at him. What I will admit was Lee's punch power was phenomenal and I saw a white flash of lightening. I was probably out for maybe 1-2 seconds but at the time I was super fit, my legs were 37 inches and I was squatting over 800lbs. As soon as I came back alive I got back up and ran at him and he tried to pick me up around the legs but he never got anywhere with it. I remember pulling his arms apart with ease because I was arguably one of the strongest people in the world at the time and Lee was a move around boxer. I knew in a grappling contest there was nobody on the planet capable of wrestling with me other than a Silverback Gorilla or a Crocodile. I just picked Lee up and threw him into the wooden doors which are still there today opposite The Station pub on Station Road. When Lee was against the wall that's when I managed to stick the nut on him and knee him a few times because I knew I couldn't use my right hand no matter how angry I was. In truth, I was fucking raging that Duffy had come up to me and punched me for fuck all, who wouldn't be?! In my opinion, it was an outright liberty but it's what he did and he was the master of knocking people out on the sneak. As me and Lee were scuffling Lee started shouting, "FAILY FAILY GET HIM OFF ME" because he was fucked and Lee knew he was trapped by my strength. He knew he had no chance of getting me off him and that's when I received the bottle of Pils across my napper which was very fortunate for Lee because I was about to bite lumps out of his face. Not only did Faily put the bottle over my head but he jumped on my back. Over the years I've heard Faily has told people, "Brian flung me off his back as easy as swatting a fly." Even though I was fighting Lee and his mate and I had my mate, Kevin didn't intervene, although I remember him saying it should only be one on to one. When me and Lee eventually made friends I remember him pointing out that at least his mate Faily had the bottle (literally) to back him up and jump on my back, unlike mine! After our scuffle me and Lee were kind of standing off each other which lasted for some time. What was in my mind at the time was that if I could get to my mates Micky Store who only lived around the corner then it could even the numbers up. Micky is no longer here as he took his own life but he was a bodybuilder who worked the doors who could really have a fight. As Lee was running at me I was trying to get to Micky's house near the police station. As me and Lee were having our handbags at dawn we were talking to each other. I was telling Lee that my finger was fucked but as we both knew the much-respected John Black that he could arrange a bare-knuckle fight between us at a later date. I do remember throwing a left hook at Lee but it missed wildly as he jumped back and even made the sound, "WOOOOOW", if it had hit him it would have taken his head off. Again I was fucking boiling calling him all the fucking arseholes under the sun and at that point, I saw a bollard at the corner of the street and I ripped it out and ran towards Lee trying to hit him with it but it only slightly clipped him, although it didn't really have much of an effect on him as he just rode the blow. I think at that point Lee had second thoughts about coming for another wrestle. I could see the look on his face as if to say, this fuckers pulling things out of the ground which no other man would have had the strength to do. At the end of it all Lee and Faily back off and I ran around to Micky Stores house and when we went back the pair were gone.

After that I made sure I trained solidly for 6 weeks but at the same time I let my finger heal. After a real training camp and when I was healed that was when I went out looking for Duffy daily. I was all over Teesside looking for Lee and lads like Paul Cook, Shaun "Nipper" Harrison, Addish, Mark and Ali Johnson and Mark Debrick could confirm this. Mark's brother Paul could have also but sadly he's no longer with us and buried not far from Lee ironically.

It was all a very long time ago but I would say the fight I had with Lee was around January 1991. Lee was shot in February so he was on crutches for all of the February and March. Lee was remanded in the April for the petrol incident with David Tapping and that's when me and him made friends at the back end of April/start of May.

I was only really close to Lee for around 12 weeks because I went to prison in early August 1991. When Lee died I'd been in for three weeks. After our fight, Lee was shot in the foot not long after and he said he wouldn't fight me because he needed time to heal and the word got back to me asking if I would wait so it would be a fair fight. I sent the word back to Duffy that he could fuck off because it wasn't fair when he smacked me on the sneak when I had a broken finger, not to mention it was also two on to one so I said he was getting it first chance I came across him.

When Lee was in jail in April on remand I was still training for him and planning on still doing him in. In fact to prove a point I started taxing people who were linked to Lee to really rub salt into the wounds. I was so psyched up to fight Duffy that I was training night and day for him and had even come down in weight because I knew Lee's strength was boxing.

I know that Lee was doing his homework on me in the time before there was going to be a rematch. I know this because he went to Bryan Flaherty's asking who this Brian Cockerill was, Bryan told him, "ooh you're fucked Lee because that kid is fucking exceptional." Also John Black had told him a bit about me so I think the full picture of what he'd got himself involved with was dawning on him. John Black told Lee straight he said he may well go on to beat me and dance rings around Cockerill "but if Brian gets hold of you you've fucking had it" not to mention he'd had his foot practically blown off quite recently so he was really an invalid. Lee was going around the people he really trusted and they all said the same to him, "if Brian grabs hold of you you're fucked" but this was something that Lee Duffy already knew too well.

At that time Lee was having his feud with me he was getting told I was doing 2000lbs leg press' which must have worried him and if it didn't he was a fool.

Going back to when I was looking for Lee in the aftermath I went to Neil Booth's girlfriend's, she told me he wasn't in but I told her to tell him that Brian Cockerill was now looking for him. At this time Paul Bryan and "Beefy" were also offering me money to go put Lee completely out of commission. At that time also Bryan and his gang were out looking for Duffy daily with a gun and that's what led to them all being arrested for the conspiracy to murder Lee Duffy and put on remand.

Another thing which must have worried Lee was he knew I'd beaten the best fighter in Redcar, Dave Williams. Williams had even beaten Eston man Peter Hoe who was probably one of the hardest men I've ever come across in my life. Hoe was super fit and if he'd fought Lee Duffy 10 times it would have been 5 – 5 with the scores he was that good. Ironically again, Hoe is also buried not far from Lee Duffy himself and in the next plot is Peter's younger brother Robbie who passed in 2019.

Going back to me fighting Dave Williams, everybody was scared of Dave, he was like the Mike Tyson of Redcar but that was who I was talking about on the Donal Macintyre documentary when I popped his eye.

One story I do know is when Paul Bryan and co were looking for Lee with guns, when they caught him they were shouting that they were going to shoot him, only for Lee to tell them, "sack all them veins, screaming and shouting, I'm here so come and do it." This happened in Brian Charrington's garage behind The Buccaneer in North Ormesby but, in my opinion, they all shit themselves. Bryan and co had sawn the shotgun in half but couldn't do it at the final minute. George Fawcett the bodybuilder was there that day to back that story up. At one time Paul Bryan was extremely close to Lee, he couldn't go through with killing him. Bryan even asked me to sort Lee when I was in Nipper Harrison's.

Another time I was in Nippers and Duffy turned up but I was hid just behind a wall and he wouldn't come in. Lee had an incredible sixth sense like no one I've ever met. When I became friends with Lee he told me he knew I was in the house and that's why he didn't go in. Let me tell you now, if you think that Lee Duffy was just a thick thug then you couldn't be as far from the truth. He really was a switched-on fella but he didn't use his head.

That time I was hid behind the wall in Nippers I was thinking that if I can get him in here then he's got no room to move and it will just be a wrestling match and it wouldn't have been a fight. Lee's best in the gym lifting was 300lbs and when we were friends I used to laugh at him telling him that's what I warm up on. I would finish on lifting 600lbs.

To make this absolutely clear I knew I couldn't have beaten Duffy in a boxing match, nobody could because he was that good. I could fight for fun but I knew Duffy was far too fast for me at 17st 9lbs. That was the heaviest Lee ever got and that was after Craig Howard got him on the gear (steroids) because when Lee was released from prison in May 1990 he was only 15st 7lbs.

Going back to when I was looking for Lee, I went to see one of Lee's good friends Mark, and me and Mark started taxing the dealers together which really pissed Lee off and believe me that was the plan.

In the March of 1991 when me and Lee were going to fight he went into Wickers World on Albert Road and broke bouncer Peter Wilson's neck on the sly which really infuriated me. I told the doormen Paul Debrick and little Guna (now sadly passed) if they ever saw Duffy in there then to call me straight away and I'd go down and get him.

A few times I would go into the town looking for Duffy but he was that elusive and usually he wouldn't even go out and show up until the stroke of midnight like a vampire. A few doormen at that time in Teesside used to say around midnight was, "the hour of The Duff" then Lee would party the night away in the blues.

I did go to see Peter Wilson, the poor bastard, in hospital. Lee had smacked him with a can of Red Stripe and broke his neck and the lad was in hospital for over a month for doing fuck all. I gave Peter my business card and told him not to worry as I was going to deal with Duffy ASAP when I came across him. I really felt for Peter Wilson as he was laid there at the hands of Duffy and it only made my hatred for Duffy burn.

In April 1991 that was when Duffy was remanded and I went to Duffy's home, 6 Durham Road in Eston, which he shared with his girlfriend Lisa but that's when I was told he was inside. I must have went maybe 3-4 times and that's when I first met Duffy's girlfriends brother Terry. Terry once told me that Lee told him that the time me and Lee had a fight that I was too strong for him. Terry's a lovely kid I've got a lot of time for him. Lee told that story to our mutual friend from Stokesley Dicky Dido that after I hit him he got up like a raging bull and that I had a head like a block of stone.

I became friends with Lee at the end of April 1991 and I'll tell you how we became very close for May/June/July 1991. Because I would train every day in 1991 I would carry a kit bag around with me but Lee told me he thought I carried a gun in it. One day I was in The Kings Head, Grangetown with Mark Johnson when the pub gets a call asking for me. Lee had just got out of jail for the petrol incident, which in my opinion was ridiculous, to spend the week on remand like he did when somebody tried to set him on fire. Anyway I got the call and by that point I was obsessed with Lee Duffy. When I was training I saw his face on the bag and when I went to sleep at night he was on my mind. Even my girlfriend at the time wanted me to fight Duffy again because she was sick of hearing about Lee Duffy. When I first fought Lee I was just under 24st but I purposely came down a few stones because I knew he was so much faster than me. That time when I threw the wild left hook he moved out of the way with ease like the Matrix and I'm no slouch myself. What I'd like to point out to you reading this is all the razzmatazz that is stuck to Lee Duffy is no bullshit. He really was that special and you're talking about the best fighter in Britain on the streets at the time. Lee Duffy was the ultimate boxer/streetfighter rolled into one and he was a bad man with it.

I find it amazing now looking back that me and him only had one fight because after our first fight we were both looking for each other for such a long time. More so me because Lee was nursing bullet wounds, but one day I saw him in the Teesside Magistrates court. I was up for something and so was Duffy, Lee really was there every other day but usually, nobody would turn up for his trials and he'd walk.

Something that really sticks out in my mind was around six weeks after our first fight when I was stood outside of the courts and Lee Duffy drove past me with a pair of shades on like Chips (the old police series) and he had his mouth open. That was one of the things I remember about Duffy was that he always seemed to have his mouth open which made him look a bit simple and gormless but he was far from it. Anyway, as soon as I saw him I shouted, "COME ON THEN" and waved his car over but he failed to come over and drove past. At that exact moment, I knew that Lee Duffy was having second thoughts about fighting me by the look on his face. When I'd finished shouting at Lee's car I went back inside and saw that Lee and Stewy Duffy, who he was also with in the car, were both supposed to be up in court too that day.

Again, and looking back with hindsight now, it was maybe because he had half his foot blown off and he was resting but I'd definitely given him food for thought and he knew he couldn't beat me and if he could he'd have had to be 100% fit and he wasn't. Another thing I only found out a long time after that was when Lee saw me at the courts he thought it was Viv Graham looking for him. Obviously, Lee had only seen me once and although I was 4 inches taller than Viv we were both extremely muscular with jet black hair.

In regards to The Duffer and Viv Graham and what really went on this is what Lee told me from his own mouth and he was usually very honest. He told me he went up to Newcastle on a Sunday evening on his own but he met up with Stephen and Michael Sayers and the rest of them and they approached a nightclub called Macy's Bar. When Lee got there he saw several of Viv's best guys minding the place and one of them said, "you're not getting in here Duffy" then the next thing 'BANG-BANG-BANG' and he put the full lot to sleep. Lee then battered them all, sparing one as long as he sent his boss a message. Lee said, "I'll let you stay awake but tell Graham The Duffers been," then he went to another of Viv's doors which Stuy Watson, Geoff Brown and Stevie Hammer were on and they just let him in even though he was wearing just a pair of shorts. When Lee was inside he began dancing all-over on tables, doing one-legged squats which he always did as well as shadow boxing on the dance floor and nobody went near him.

Another night Lee was in Newcastle and he slapped an ex-boxer by the name of Howard Mills who'd not long before that been shot on the Quayside. Howard was on the door where Lee went to in Newcastle but when Lee got there he told the bouncer (pointing to his leg) that he got that for being a grass and he said, "here there's a slap off the Duffer" and he banged him across the mouth with an open palm in front of the full club. The bouncer had others there but nobody came forward to back him up and Duffy was just on his own. Lee would do things like that to make a statement across Tyneside as if to say, "does anybody else want a fucking go?"

That time Lee hit me he was that fast I didn't even see it coming and he always seemed to have his feet in place like the perfect boxer. Another thing about Lee Duffy was he was a fabulous dancer and he could do squats on one leg then come back up like the Russian Polska dancers.

The day I made friends with Lee I was in The Kings Head, straight away before I answered the phone for some reason I knew it was Lee Duffy. To this day I didn't even know how he knew I was in Trevor Thirlwell's pub but he did. Then again Lee did have his little spies and no doubt somebody reported back to him. As soon as I heard Lee's softly spoken Boro accent I told him that me and him needed to get it on and that I'd fight him on the moon if he wanted it but he surprised me by what he went on to say. Lee told me he was ringing up to apologise. Lee said it was wrong what he had done to me and that it was all Faily's fault because he was winding him up, plus he was off his head on gear. Lee asked me if he could come and see me but I told him to fuck off and I wasn't interested in his setups but Lee promised me on his daughters life he was genuine and he would behave so the plan was to go to Lee's house with Mark. Still, I wasn't convinced and it did make me think that Lee had made our mutual friend Mark bring me to him for an ambush. I think I even may have said to Mark beforehand, and I think the words I used were, "if you've set me up with him I'll fucking kill you ya cunt." In the end,

I ended up going to Lee's Mam's home at 24, Keir Hardie Crescent which was the Duffy family home that Lee had grown up in. As I walked in Lee was sat in the chair but he was very much like he was on that famous photo when he's bending over tying his shoelace with his mouth open. As I walked in with Mark Lee shouted, "sit down Brian," then he turned to his mother Brenda and said, "look at the fucking size of him. I must have been mad wanting to fight someone the size of him."

A little while later Lee's best mate Neil Booth turned up and I could read his face when he saw me in Lee's Mams as if to say, what the fucks going on here! I know this sounds almost like what little boys do in the playground but that day in that front room in Keir Hardie Crescent Lee said to me, "there's my hand and there's my heart and I promise you Brian that I'll never fight you again" and he shook my hand. I did shake his hand but I still didn't trust him one bit as the saying goes, once bitten twice shy, so I thought 'I'll be keeping a close fucking eye on you mate.' We're not talking about your average man here in Lee Duffy, I'm talking about a man who could destroy you and all your faculties with one punch. You've only got to look at what Lee did with lads such as Dave Woodier. Even though Lee's arms were maybe 17-18 inches compared to my 23-24 inches the man's power was as deadly as it was humanely possible for a man to be.

That day me and Lee put our history behind us and we went straight to Redcar taxing drug dealers and we made £1500 between us. Before Lee Duffy showed me this new job in how to tax drug dealers I'd been making £136 per week doing the doors, whereas now I'd just made literally hundreds in one day. After that day out with Lee Duffy, I thought, fuck this working the doors lark I'm going to become a full-time taxman. That day in Redcar there was me, Lee, Boothy and Mark and we just laughed all day as well at Lee's crazy antics.

Although taxing drug dealers is the most dangerous job in the world Lee Duffy made it look easy. I, of course, did it for decades but I did my apprenticeship with the best in Lee Duffy. The three months of working alongside Lee taught me everything I needed to know in that game.

Back in taxing though in 1991 there were none of the big drugs that there would go on to be. Maybe there was a bit of very expensive cocaine but it was all mainly cannabis. One lad me and Lee got in Redcar who'd said he was going to do all sorts to us we took a lot of money off him and ended up kidnapping him in an old Granada. Boothy was driving and there was me and Lee but Mark got him in the car and as he got him in he hit him very half-heartedly. Lee saw it and rolled his eyes in embarrassment as if to say, if you're going to hit him then do it properly. Lee Duffy was a very funny man without even realising he was and he had some funny mannerisms. Lee told Mark the punch he hit him with wasn't worth the effort but he did raise his eyebrows in approval when I grabbed the lad and threatened to break his kneecaps with a hammer I had in my hand. It was done to scare him for his money but me and Lee took this man down the Gare on Redcar beach and told him what we wanted and it worked a treat, because when we took him back to where we got him from he walked into his Mam's guesthouse and then came out with £1000 in notes. After we did that one we went on to do more jobs like that and don't forget this was the very first day me and Lee had even made friends. After that me and Lee were together for five or six days a week for the next three months. Even the days Mark wouldn't stay out all day, me and Lee just loved it and our lust for other people's money was what fuelled our searches for the bad guys of Teesside.

That night when I got home my girlfriend at the time asked me what had gone on, I told her that Lee had shook my hand and we went on to have a very financially rewarding day but my girlfriend told me I was being silly letting my guard down. She told me I was mad to trust Duffy, but something inside me told me it was ok this time.

Another thing that Lee's sister Louise told me after Lee's death was that Lee had been to see her and told her that he was going to make friends with this Brian Cockerill. Although Lee had six siblings it was Louise who he was always the closest to. Louise told me that she used to wind Lee up saying that he was scared of me because he'd never wanted to make friends with anyone in his whole life after a fight. I think Lee was worried about facing me again and that's not me blowing my own trumpet. Lee knew at almost 24st I was somebody he wasn't used to coming across. Louise told me how Lee told her how ridiculously strong I was and that when I grabbed hold of him he was fucked. Not to mention Lee had people in his ear like Bryan Flaherty, Tommy Harrison and John Black and these were proper men in the eyes of the Duff who he trusted greatly.

Lee actually did tell me when we became friends that those people also said to him that Brian was a lovely guy so why do you even want to be fighting with the likes of him when there are lowlife drug dealers out there who were plotting to kill him.

When I became friends with Lee Duffy I would say we were inseparable for the twelve or so weeks that we worked together but he was a sod. He even hit my best mate Ossie Bingham for fuck all but that was the man.

I know the bodybuilder Craig Howard was well put out by Lee when we became friends and not enemies. In my opinion, Craig Howard was one of those people who liked to be seen with all the best fighters like your Lee Duffy's, Dave Williams and then he made a beeline for me. I found Craig very manipulative and clever with it. Regarding having a brain he was years ahead of me and Lee Duffy put together. Not to mention he was about seven or eight years older than us. I'd been with Craig when he's asked me to drive him to places and he'd ask me to wait outside, then when he was outside he'd go into a house and demand money by telling them he had Brian Cockerill ready to come in and kick off unless he was paid X amount of money. Then he'd come back to me and tell me he was taking me for a £20 meal but wouldn't tell me he'd just made £500 by using my name in the first place. Although Craig was a very impressive bodybuilder he was just a shit stirrer who couldn't fight sleep and that's why he hung around Duffy so much. I remember John Graham offering him out and Craig ran away saying he was going to fight him tomorrow but it was always all bullshit with Craig. I had crack cocaine a lot with Lee Duffy but I had it with Craig more. It was really Craig Howard who got Duffy on it in the first place. In fact, it was how Craig died. He'd been smoking crack in a caravan and he went to go to the toilet and then his Mrs heard a loud bang and the next thing she knew was he'd collapsed and had a heart attack.

We weren't always friends me and Craig because I once knocked him out breaking his nose and took his car off him. I even took the coat which was Lee's off him that day. I told him he wasn't even worthy to own Lee Duffy's coat and I still have it today. When Lee died I began hanging around with Craig and that's really how I became a crackhead but that's another story which we'll talk about later.

Craig used to tell me he'd say, "Brian when you take drugs you're alright but eventually you'll get paranoid and once you get paranoid you'll always get it." Craig was a very clever guy and knew what he was talking about. Another thing Craig used to say is when you're so intelligent and you take coke and then you take too much of the stuff you start imagining things that people not as bright would do.

The one thing I noticed about my friendship with Lee was he never liked to sleep in the same house for more than two days in a row. Lee used to say, "Brian that's how people end up being killed and your enemies can read your routine" and he was right. Lee Duffy was a master at what he did and he was a very elusive man to pin down. It's the reason why I could never find him when we were enemies. Lee's sleeping arrangements were at Boothy's, Vince Agar's, Faily's, Lisa's, his sister Louise's etc… I did take Lee to meet my girlfriend at home and she, in the end, fell for his charms because he was such a likeable lad and nothing like what you read about him if you met him even just once.

Lee used to like taking me up Stokesley or as he used to call it, "out in the sticks" because it gave him a break from everybody out to kill him like they were in Middlesbrough. Lee was quite close to a fella named Dicky Dido from there. I think a lot of it was to do with Lee being barred out of Teesside so that's why he would go to the little places just outside of Middlesbrough like Stokesley in the first place and even places like Whitby.

One day I was up there drinking in Stokesley and I was in the company of Dido and this right tit who kept on saying to me that I should knock Lee Duffy out when Lee was at the toilet. So, Dido himself got up and sparked the sneaky gobshite with a body shot and dropped him.

Lee did take me to his house that he shared with Lisa and I held his baby daughter. In fact, there is one picture, which is quite famous, of Lee holding his baby daughter, I was there when that was taken. One of the things I'll never forget when he had hold of his daughter was him saying to me, "on her life me and you will never fight again and that's my word to you." I've never forgotten that.

It must have been a funny sight because sometimes we'd drive about in this tiny little Panda car which must have been funny to see considering the size of me and him. A lot of the time Lee was on the run from the law but he was never edgy about seeing the police. The man just didn't give a fuck.
Lee took me to the old Middlesbrough club owner Freddie Vasey's house a few times in Coulby Newham who was a lovely man. Another one who I met through Lee was Terry Dicko who always seemed to be messing about playing practical jokes and couldn't be serious for more than five seconds. Another guy I also met was the MC Lee Harrison who used to tell me and Lee, divided we stand and divided we fall.

As MC Lee would always be shouting, "FIRE," he would always say how me and Lee could run the fucking world.

Every day me and Lee were out meeting all kinds of interesting characters. We were glued at the hip for those three months and obsessed with making money.

Lee did have some funny ways though and I can't think of any more bonkers than the time we came out of the old café on Linthorpe Road which was Roy's. As we were coming back from having breakfast we saw this guy, he wasn't a traffic warden, he was one of those wheel clampers and he'd put the clamp on Lee Duffy and Brian Cockerill's car. You should have seen his face when Lee shouted, "OI OI GET THAT OFF THERE NOW!" Well, the lad looked up and if it wasn't bad enough that he'd just clamped Lee Duffy's car he had Brian Cockerill stood with him. Again Lee shouted to him, "GET THAT OFF OR I'LL GET BRIAN TO RIP IT OFF." The wheel clampers words to us were, "EH EH EH... I'm sorry about that lads I'll take it off now sorry." The lad was just doing his job but he apologised to Lee and took it off. Obviously, he knew who we both were and one would have been bad but to get both of us at the same time was damn right unlucky. I wonder if that lad is telling that story in a Teesside pub somewhere!

One of the things Lee Duffy used to do was take me to places to show off. He'd constantly be asking me to show people just how strong I was by lifting people's cars off the floor. I'd have to say to him, "Lee will you wrap in asking me to lift cars up for people." I suppose it was my party piece but he'd be asking me maybe three or four times a day. What I used to do was get two beermats to protect my hands and I'd lift peoples cars off the floor 5/6 times. I used to do it for Lee a few times up Stokesley, Dicky Dido will remember. One day I did it and Lee's best mate Neil Booth had a go but nearly broke his fucking neck doing it (laughs).

Another thing Lee was a bastard for is never buying petrol. One day he took a car off someone and he left it over the border at the side of the road. Another time he took a car off another lad which was a convertible and when he put the hood up and he'd got to 70mph it blew off and he just started laughing and continued driving and dancing at the same time to the loud music.

Lee used to ask my advice on getting bigger and he wanted to train with me and Craig Howard. One day I was in the gym with Lee and Craig in Les Moore's gym over Stockton and I knew Lee was trying to impress me by putting more and more plates on the bar but as he was doing that, he could only get one rep whereas I did twelve or something more ridiculous. I used to warm up on what Lee's best was. I'm not bragging but those are facts and Paul Epstein the old weightlifter who's in his 70s now was there. He could confirm that story. Sometimes Lee would put large sums on these bars and struggle to do one where I could do 20 and he used to be gobsmacked.

The words Lee Duffy used to use all the time to describe me was of me having, "hideous strength." It was something he always said a lot. Sometimes I used to put six plates on each end and Lee would run around everyone in the gym to come and watch, then he'd say I was doing it to take the piss out of him by showboating but I wasn't. I was just doing that every week. When we did legs with Lee I was doing 800lbs and he was doing about 300lbs. I was nearly three times stronger than him on legs.

In the three months, I spent by Lee Duffy's side I never saw him fight or bully anybody once. One day I waited in the car and Lee popped into a gym and when he came back he told me he slapped a lad in there but that was as close as it came to me seeing Lee Duffy fight as it got. Even when he fought me I didn't see the punch coming but I saw him on the bags and on the pads and the guy was dynamite and brought hell with it. As I said I got to know Terry Dicko through Lee Duffy and Lee used to always say, "Terry was a dangerous little cunt with weapons."

I was there with Lee when he got his tattoo of his girlfriend on his arm in Scorpio's. Lee gave the tattooist a photo of Lisa and it was drawn from that. While we're on the subject of tattoos me and Lee had the same devil which said, "Born to raise hell" underneath it. I had it done because my uncle Frank played for Manchester United but he had it for obvious reasons. Another uncanny story was we both got it done in the same place at Duke Webb's in Hartlepool in the same year in 1981.

Lee was forever wanting to play practical jokes on people very much like Terry Dicko, it's probably why those two got on.

Anyway about a week after me and Lee had made up Lee hatched a plan to put the shits up his mate Faily. Lee went to his house on Princess Road just across the road from Ramsey's Blues. What happened was Lee went into Faily's and told him that although him and me had made friends I was still fuming with him for being a sneaky cunt and hitting me over the head with a bottle so I was here to have a fight with him. Lee would wind Faily up for some time and when Faily looked out I shouted, "get outside here now you daft cunt because I'm going to pull your fucking head off." Well Faily was saying to Lee that he couldn't fight me and asked Lee what was he going to do. After a couple of minutes I went in and gave Faily a cuddle and told him it was all forgot about but Lee thought it was hysterical. That was him and he just loved to wind people up like that even though I kinda felt sorry for Faily it was Lee who made me do it.

Lee did show me his gunshot wounds several times. He told me it used to ache and that the blow relieved his pain. Even though he was limping and hobbling about on crutches he could still fight better than everyone.

It's been said that Lee would talk about his death all the time but I never heard him speak like that, in fact, he would say to me often that I wouldn't make thirty because I used to run at drug dealers with guns, etc… Me and Lee Duffy probably taxed not far off a hundred people in three months. We were out every day and the pair of us were hated for doing it.

When Beefy, Nipper and Bryan were plotting to kill Lee they all tried to recruit me to get Lee and Lee told me I was hoodwinked. Lee told me that those fuckers only use people whereas he would have died for me and me for him. Our time together was short lived but I think we both genuinely realised just how genuine people we were and I'm glad we never had the other fight which was planned as either one of us could have died.

When the author Jamie Boyle has sat down with me to help me write this book there are so many stories that have come back to me which I'd forgotten for over a quarter of a century. Like the time I was out looking for Lee Duffy with Mark Johnson and Nipper Harrison was driving and we saw him in a green Sierra with Craig Howard near where he lived at the bottom of Durham Road. As we saw Duffy I shouted, "THERE HE IS" and I made Nipper follow his car. At the time I had a pair of army boots on as John Black always told me when I worked on the door for him they were the best things to wear if you were ever going to battle. After a while of following Craig Howards car with Duffy in, Craig was a shit hot driver by the way and the best I've ever seen, I got out of the car and ran towards Duffy shouting come on then but the pair locked the door. This wasn't long after Lee had been shot and his foot was fucked so he couldn't do anything anyway. What I'm trying to say is I'm glad that nothing ever went off between me and Lee although I was very angry with him at the time.

Going back to me outside of the car, Craig's car stalled and I jumped on the back of the car but it started again and they drove off with me falling off. At the time I told people that that was Lee running away but the truth was he had one foot but that's exactly what happened. I know not long after that Lee went to Peter Hoe who was another lovely lad but could fight for fun. I'm not exaggerating but Peter Hoe would have been a close match with Lee Duffy, the kid could seriously have a fight with anyone. Peter was fitter than me and Lee and we would often go jogging up Eston Hills with rucksacks the guy was fucking super fit. I think Lee went to see Peter because when I was having trouble with Lee it was Peter who came up to me and said, "if you're going to fight Lee can you wait until his foots better Bri?" Peter Hoe was almost the mediator between us for a little while. It just shows how honest Lee Duffy was though because when Peter Hoe went back to Lee and told him what I'd said he said that every word that Brian told you is true. Peter encouraged me and Lee to make friends and the rest is history as you know.

I really liked Peter Hoe and I sat down with him one day and I told him if anyone ever said anything to you about me then please come to me and ask. I told Peter don't be like Lee Duffy who was some people's clockwork mouse. Everybody knows a certain gentleman would wind the key in Duffy's back and point him in whatever direction he wanted. Even John Black used to say the same thing to Lee's face. I've told you all that Lee Duffy was far from thick but he couldn't see the people who'd use him for their own selfish reasons. Then again Lee Duffy used to like showing off so if he knocked some guy out in a pub it would get the whole of Middlesbrough talking about him and that's what he was addicted too.

Believe it or not but the Lee Duffy I knew wasn't bad tempered considering he punched a lot of people. I tell you what Lee Duffy was, he was like one of those professional boxers like Lennox Lewis who never shouted or balled but come fight time they were switched on. That's what Duffy was about. Lee mastered the art at being calm and it was something I could never do but eventually did and it was Lee who showed me. Lee used to stay calm like a Shaolin monk. Considering there was no internet in them days back in 1991 it showed how big the beef between us was as the police even knew about it and some of them were betting on who they fancied. Even two top senior officers confirmed this to Jamie Boyle when he was researching for the Lee Duffy books. Even solicitors and barristers in Teesside would talk about it because some of them asked me in person.

Going back to when myself and Lee became friends, Lee one day told me he was glad that I worked out the people who were trying to murder him which brought a tear to my eye. Lee said, "them lads would run away from you and I'd put my life on the line for you" which is quite heart pulling even now, almost 30 years on.

Over the years I know some in Teesside have accused me of being disrespectful towards Lee Duffy because I've said I beat him in a fight. Well, the truth is I did have him beat in that fight and I had him beat mentally for the months after and Lee even admitted that to me one day when we were taking drugs together. Craig Howard and his girlfriend were there at the time. Lee told me that if it wasn't for Faily hitting me over the head with that beer bottle that he was fucked. Lee told me he knew that he couldn't have got me off him.

Lee told me that for six weeks he couldn't sleep knowing that there was somebody out there in Teesside as good as him. That's the truth on my brother's grave and people can read into that what they will. Lee told me that even his little sister Louise used to say to him, "you're worried about him aren't you because you're not scared of anyone" and Louise can confirm that today. I would often bump into Louise after Lee died at the Grangetown raves and she'd always come up to me for a cuddle she is a lovely girl.

I'd like to fully admit I learned a lot in such a short space of time from Duffy but the fact of the matter is he wasn't nice sometimes. He had that persona where he'd treat people like shit. I often heard Lee saying to people, "ERE YOU MOVE DOYLE" and I'd say to Lee that they're human as well Lee but his attitude was they were daft.

Lee had a nasty side, I'd be lying if I said he didn't. Like once he had a group of lads against the wall in Parkend at Penrith Shops and he took all their giro's off them and cashed them. The fact of the matter with my friend Lee was that he was dragged up and didn't know any different. After he stole all the lads' dole, "I said to him Lee that's fucking wrong man" but he told me that they were only going to waste it on drugs, but I said, "well that's only what you're going to do with it!" It was funny in one way but it wasn't if you know what I mean. I said to him imagine if somebody came and took your money off you but all he said was, "nobody will come and do that to me" but I said, "Lee you're missing the point."

I don't think I ever saw Lee pay for a taxi in his life and sometimes he'd make the drivers take him to Newcastle to see the Sayers. I would tell Lee it didn't matter how hard we both were it was always nice to be nice but he'd just laugh and say I was soft and that I was talking crap. Lee wouldn't ever think that he had to wait his turn at pool or for phones in jail whereas anybody who's ever come into my personal space knows that's what Brian Cockerill was about. Lee had this view that he was Lee Duffy and he ran Middlesbrough.

At the end of Lee's life, he thought he was a robot like the Terminator and he couldn't be killed no matter what. When you were around Lee Duffy like I was or Neil Booth, Vince Agar or Terry Dicko you could tell that's what came off him in abundance towards the end. If you want me to sum it up for you he believed his own hype but the man wasn't hype if that makes sense. He was the real deal in a fighting sense but he was only human. Lee had this thing that nobody could beat him and when he eventually joined forces with me he became twice as powerful.

Every day he would be with me and everyday it would be, "NOW THEN NOW THEN BIG FELLA" and he would cuddle me daily. I don't think there was a day that I spent in Lee's company where he didn't, at least once, give me a hug. Lee used to tell me that in a fighting sense he'd put me up against anyone in this country and that was Lenny McLean and Paul Sykes included.

If anyone read the story of Lenny McLean fighting Lee Duffy in the Steve Richards books then that was 100% true because it was Tommy Harrison behind it pulling the strings. In my opinion, I don't think Lenny would have stood a chance against the Duffer as Lenny had over 20 years on him and was finished by then. In fact, Lee was that good he'd have beaten a prime McLean in my eyes but that's just my opinion. Lee used to say to me that I myself could be beat in the ring but not on the streets because once I've got hold of someone they can't punch you if you've got hold of them. Lee used to say, "Brian I can only bench 300lbs but you're doing 600lbs and nobody in the worlds doing that".

There was one particular time when Lee got me fucked on drugs in The Havana and I started thinking he was going to start on me. Lee gave me an E tablet and I didn't know what was happening. In truth I only had half whereas Lee was an E monster and could handle them. Well twenty minutes later I was off my boiler and Lee was up dancing with Terry Dicko doing all these mad high kicks and I was a shivering mess. Terry reminds me of Klunk from The Wacky Races because of all the little tics he has and him and Lee were causing mayhem and just generally having a good time but I was declining rapidly and my head was battered. I was utterly cabbaged and now I started thinking that Duffy was going to do me in and I'd have been 100% at his mercy but he couldn't have been more opposite. I was convinced that Lee was about to use me as a human sacrifice but the only thing he did to me was grab me and give me a cuddle and told me he was going to look after me. "Are you alright mate?" Lee asked, I told him I wasn't and I felt fucking weird and then Lee picked me up in an army pose and marched me to the front door where he got Craig Howard to pick me up. Lee virtually carried me like we were dodging bombs in Vietnam and he took me to Bryan Flaherty's flat were we had a few vodka's. I managed to come around via nurse Duffy and Lee got Flaherty fucked and we played cards. Lee loved Flaherty's. Sadly Bryan passed a couple of years ago. The one thing I would say about Lee was if you got into his close circle of friends such as Faily or Boothy then he'd have done anything for you and you could say anything to him. I know when I used to leave Lee on a night that he'd been ready to go off on his crack cocaine binges. At that time I wasn't really on the crack then but I know that drug caused Lee a lot of his paranoia and I've been the same. One minute you're having the best time of your life and then the next your searching for bits in the carpets and smoking old toenails and dog hairs.

In early August I ended up going to prison for around ten weeks. I'd had a fight with a guy named Ste Murphy on Redcar Sea Front. I'd saw him kicking a little lad from South Bank called Mono or something so I ran over and stopped the fight until Murphy punched me in the face and it was the worst thing he could have ever done because I went all out on him and he got the beating of his life. To cut a long story short the coppers came and it took them 90 minutes to get me in the van. Then when I was in I kicked the van door hinges off and got out to riot against them again. I had another little scrape against Ste Murphy who was a big man by the way not long after. He came out of a pizza shop and ran at me and I punched him and lifted him off the floor and broke his jaw. Murphy ended up making a statement against me and I was charged and arrested. The funny thing was the morning I was arrested there must have been maybe thirty police officers who surrounded my house in their dozens just to take me in. Another time I was arrested it was put on hold because Cleveland police only had eleven coppers on the shift and they needed more. Anyway, that's why I ended up losing my liberty for the ten weeks when Lee Duffy died.

When Lee died I'd been locked up for about three weeks on remand in Durham jail. When I was in Durham I became a right handful for the screws and I would inspect them daily. If one needed a shave I'd point it out or if one's boots needed polishing I'd pull them on it like a General in the British Army. If ever the screws came to my cell it was the MUFTI squad in riot shields, truncheons and helmets. At that time in my life I had nothing but attitude for the screws of Durham jail and spent a long time in the block. Funnily enough my old pal Elvis Tomo came in next door to me so we had a catch up on old times.

Now, this may sound farfetched but it's the truth and you can think what you want but on the other side of my cell was David Tapping who was in for throwing the petrol over Lee Duffy in The Commercial pub. I didn't know David but I knew his brother Tony from working the doors but I'll never forget Tapping's words as long as I live. "Bri, Lee Duffy's dead" David Tapping shouted from his cell on that Sunday morning. Straight away I thought fucking bullshit because of all the people in the whole prison for it to come from it had to be complete bullshit because it came from him. When I found out it was true I was so upset because at the time he was one of my best friends. I asked to go to his funeral but it was a straight "NO" back from the governor. My memories of that time 29 years ago were of me just sat on association reading it in The Gazette and The Northern Echo. Seeing his pictures in the paper and feeling fucking heartbroken that my friend was gone. When I got out I never went to his grave. In fact, I'd never been to his grave until I started writing this book and I went with the author Jamie Boyle and my brother Bobby. I don't believe you have to go to people's graves if you've been good to them in life. I know I've seen a lot of two-faced cunts who hated Lee but when he died have been like a fly around shit around his grave. When I was with Lee he was my friend and I wanted to remember him that way.

It was hard when the lowlifes smashed his grave up several times and after he died they were having parties which made me fucking puke. It's just so so sad that he had to die but it was inevitable it was going to happen. Lee used to say to me, "Bri I can go in a pub and I can empty it in thirty seconds" but I used to tell him that wasn't clever but he'd just smile. I would tell him that I could walk into a pub and fill it!

I honestly used to say to Lee "you used to get bullied as a kid so why do you want to be like that?" But he never used to answer me! By the way, I used to get bullied just as much as him you know! I got it really bad because when I came to Teesside I still had my Scottish accent, not to mention that I couldn't walk properly and I couldn't read and write properly either because of my dyslexia. Six lads used to beat me up every day for about a year and it wasn't until about 13 that I started fighting back so Lee should have known better.

When Lee used to take taxi drivers cars off them for days I'd say, "Lee that's bullying mate and those men have to work for their families."

When Lee was with me he was brilliant but when he wasn't he was doing horrible things and people were hating him for it. I know for a fact that if I'd have been there when Lee died he wouldn't have been killed that night! I'd have been straight in and grabbed that knife because that's the type of person I am. I've never ever slagged Lee Duffy off in life but at one of my book launches in 2005 one of Lee's daughters came to heckle me and have a go at me and I always found that very unfair because I loved her dad.

The fact of the matter is, and however short it was, that Lee Paul Duffy was a huge part of my life. I didn't ask for him to come and punch me in the face that day in Redcar. I was just a nice lad walking down a street and he punched me in the face for nothing. Lee only did that because I was a big man and he wanted to knock me out so it could enhance his reputation.

Even though I knew Lee Duffy would be killed at some point I would like to say that no human being should have died the way he did.

Over the years I've spoken to the man who held Lee as he died who I've never had one crossed word over the years with, he's a lovely big lad but told me that he was talking to Lee and telling him not to close his eyes. That man was loyal to Lee and was by his side and for that, the man who stayed with Lee, deserves total respect. Don't ever forget also that poor man who held Lee as he died lost a huge chunk of himself when Lee Duffy died in his arms in the back of that car before he arrived at the old General Hospital.

You know my first book 'The Taxman' with Steve Richards covered the story about how I got attacked by eleven men with guns, baseball bats etc in Tommy Harrison's house so I don't want to cover old ground. What I do want to tell you is when I was being beaten to a pulp which led to me receiving over 170 stitches in 1992 I was thinking of Lee Duffy. When I was on the floor being kicked the shit out of I'll never forget thinking, just keep your eyes open and don't die. When I was on the floor and the savages were around me Lee came into my thoughts god rest him. I'll never forget thinking, 'this is what it must have been like for Lee Duffy', as my life was flashing before my own eyes and I thought I was about to meet my final fate.

I'll tell you another story about Lee which he told me from his own mouth. He told me one day he was in Walton jail not far from his release date and he was just about to go on a visit with his girlfriend Lisa and Robert Suggett. He was only minutes away from walking out into the visiting room when they put a sex offender near Lee so he laid him out. As soon as he did that Lee turned and did a couple of screws but was eventually overpowered by about twelve of them. I'm not kidding you, Lee told me, he said "Brian every one of them kicked the shit out of me. I was that beaten I just curled up in a ball and cried myself to sleep and that was the lowest point of my life." I spoke with John Black also and Lee told him that exact same story. The point I'm trying to make was even the big invincible Lee Paul Duffy was only human but I heard that from Lee's mouth myself.

I know sometimes a lot of people used to use Lee. Sometimes drug dealers who had loads of gear in themselves would grass other local dealers up to The Duffer so he'd go and hunt them down and then that party would be left alone.

I wish my friend was still here now. R.I.P The Duffer you were truly a one off and Middlesbrough will never forget your name.

"Often people would come to me and say, oh Brian he owes me 10K but it's not the money it's the principal, I would always smile and tell them, well you keep the principal and I'll just keep the money."

Brian Cockerill

CHAPTER 7

COCKERILL SECURITY

For many years I worked the doors around Teesside with Mark Johnson and Addish and it ended up with me getting almost every door in Teesside, that's how Cockerill Security came about. Although my name was above the proprietors, I had around thirty men all working for me. It was a properly fully licenced and lucrative company but of course, I fucked it all up didn't I. Although Ellwood & Hoyle took over and became the biggest door security in the North I had all the contracts before them and I only have myself to blame for losing my empire. I had doors over Redcar, Billingham, Seaton Crew, Hartlepool and other places but I let it all go to rack and ruins through the drugs. I suppose at the time my thinking was that the security was only making me a couple of grand a month and at the time with me taxing drug dealers I was earning more than that in one day. It's only now as I've gotten older that I realise I threw my empire away because my name was huge with the Steve Richards book and 'The Taxman' documentary. I mean my name was massive anyway in Teesside but after the pair came out in 2005 and 2006 it put me on another level. It wasn't only the pubs and clubs that Cockerill Security did, I'd started doing shops for maybe just £25 a week but I accumulated a load. These days that kind of security doesn't exist anymore because the man has been replaced by a robot. Companies know it's cheaper to stick a camera there 24/7 and it links directly to the police station. My company security boards were bright luminous yellow which screamed out hazardous and KEEP OUT! It's funny because when I used to put my business security boards all over the estates I found they'd always go missing. At first, I thought it was the police, then I thought it may be other local security companies taking them down but it was the young kids from across the estates of Teesside and they'd stick them on their walls at home. Some even would put them on their bedroom walls or just there mam and dad's shed. As I've told you my whole business collapsed because when I was supposed to be going around to visit these sites I wasn't turning up because I was on a comedown from the crack. I'll even admit that I was asking for more payments in advance which is a big no-no in business and that's how my security company fell apart. It was my own doing and nobody else's. It wasn't always money though that I looked after these businesses for though, sometimes I would be paid with kebabs. I know it sounds daft but I'd be eating out for free on healthy chicken kebabs twice a week and the owners would be happy that that was the only payment they had to make to be able to tell people that he was looked after by Brian Cockerill. Indians, Chinese and other takeaways also did the same and paid me in food. Even now after all these years I still see my company signs up on some people's businesses as if to say I'm looking after it. In the making of this book somebody sent my Facebook page a picture of a Cockerill Security sign in Pontefract, I never had any contracts in Pontefract ever so there you go! On a Friday when I'd be out collecting and they'd be brown envelopes with huge wads of cash and it would be all gone by the Monday and all spent in some crack den.

During my Cockerill Security days, I never had an office like you see some of these companies I just worked from home. Bryan Flaherty, God rest his soul, used to say to me, "Brian if I had your name I'd be a fucking billionaire." It was the same for Lee Duffy wasn't it. Then again with Lee, I don't think he'd have ever calmed down enough to want to be a businessman he just wanted to party, fight, take narcotics and be the talk of the town. I think, regarding the security companies, it's finished as I said about the cameras. You can buy a camera from £30 and that does exactly what you're paying a guard to do on the national minimum wage. That one video camera, in fact, can look after ten building sites and if there's anything dodgy about to happen then a loudspeaker shouts, "GET OFF THIS FORECOURT OR WE WILL PHONE THE POLICE" and the jobs done. You can't beat something as efficient as that.

Also, the day of the knuckle draggers are gone in pubs. Through the 1980s in Teesside if you were a psychotic GBH merchant with a bald head and tattoos that helped you get a job, these days it's all S.I.A carded guys who work alongside the police. It's the same with drugs and people ask me why I don't do the taxing anymore and I tell them that there's nobody to tax.

In Middlesbrough, there are hundreds of drug dealers with an ounce here and there. Back in my day, I could steal 20 kilo of blow and I'd get about 30 grand in one lump sum from it.

"People sleep peaceably in their beds at night only because rough men stand ready to do violence on their behalf".

George Orwell

CHAPTER 8

REGRETS AND WHAT IF'S!

After the heights of the book and documentary, I came crashing down to earth. I was still plodding away and being very successful at business but I was a full blown crackhead. Any money that I made during the day me and Amanda would spend it on crack on the night. If you Google the name Brian Cockerill one of the first things that comes up from the search engine is the "Cockerill twitch" and I developed that from the drugs that I was taking.

If anyone meets me today then one of the first things you'll notice about me is it's gone. I don't have them tics today in 2020. When you take any types of substance you get a twitch because that's your nervous system being shot to fuck. Don't get me wrong there's people out there with mental health problems and it can be from that but what I had was 100% from the drugs.

In 2008 and 2009 I was still very much up and down dealing with my brother's death and how I used to deal with that is to take the crack. My brother hung himself because he was raped as a child and I never ever knew that until I was told that it was in his suicide note, which made me blame myself. I was always out helping strangers and sorting their issues out but I didn't help my brother when he was going through his own turmoil. For years my brother skinny took heroin to take his problems away and I could never understand the reason until after his death. I used to scream at him to get off that shite he was taking. I know some of you will be thinking that's a bit rich coming from a crackhead like Brian Cockerill but I've never taken heroin in my life. It still hurts today that none of our family knew that my brother Peter Thomas Cockerill had been raped as a kid and also in prison. I've never read his suicide note to this day because it's always been too upsetting for me to deal with. I know one of the last things he said in the note was for me to look after his son but why couldn't he tell me what had happened to him? I could have gone and got the people back for him and made it better.

At the end of 2006 when my brother took his own life, he'd carried this dark secret around with him for his whole life and never told anyone and it breaks my heart for me to think of this. He was my little brother and I would have died for him. My brother skinny, just before his death, had done really well coming off the smack and we were all proud of him for doing it. He'd been staying with me for a couple of days before. I think he left mine on the Wednesday and he hung himself on the Friday and none of us had any inclination whatsoever. When he left my house on that day he was in such high spirits and telling me how much he loved me for helping him. I know that after my brother's death that people were saying it was my fault because I must have gotten him on the crack and he's hung himself on the comedown etc etc blah blah but it proved that was rubbish when the coroner did the autopsy on my brothers body and it was found that there was nothing in his system.

I know I seem to be blaming the drugs for all the things in life that I've failed to do but when I lost my little brother the way I did at the end of 2006 just before my documentary was aired I just lost the will to live. For the years of 2007/08/09 I threw some seriously good offers away from Steve Richards, Donal Macintyre and even one to appear in a Guy Ritchie film. I should have been doing jobs like looking after the likes of Madonna in the West End of London for £2,000 a night but as I've said for years my head came off and I blew it all.

I even, at one point, got an agent called Tony Nunn whose one liner was, "I'm second to Nunn to the stars." His wife used to be a big singing star through the 60s and Tony had some proper connections and was worth about 60 million himself. Tony made contact with me through watching my documentary and he told me he was intrigued by my life story. My good friend Sean could back that story up as Sean was with me when I went to meet Tony in a café in Saltburn. At that time I was still out taxing and getting people's things back for 50% of the debt. If someone was owed maybe £10,000 from bad people then the chances are without getting me involved they'd never see a penny of that back again, whereas if they got Brian Cockerill involved they knew I'd recover the full sum and they'd then be getting at least £5,000 back. That was just how that system worked and it got around by word of mouth.

It's not something that you could put in the Yellow Pages is it, as the notorious Yorkshire debt collector Paul Sykes would say! I would get people who'd say, "aah well Brian can I just give you £2,000" but I'd tell them that was my fixed price and they came around to my way of thinking. Half a loaf was better than no loaf as they say eh. Bearing in mind I would usually be the last option and these people had already been to the police and the courts, in fact, I could have demanded 80% but I was a fair man.

I know the legendary East Ender Roy Shaw would get a job like that and keep 100% of what he got back. He would then go back to the third party and tell them, "I'll back you up with them for life but it's mine. I've saved your face son." I didn't work like that although I was more than capable.

Another thing I would do is take Amanda along on every job I did which might sound bizarre but I'll tell you why I used to do it. Amanda had never been in trouble in her life so if I needed a witness then she was credible. Also if I was ever pulled by the police and they were trying to pin something on me like demanding money with menaces then my solicitor would be able to ask, "why would Brian Cockerill take his Mrs on a job which could have got him shot?" I taught Amanda well in psychology and she was so good at it. Sometimes she would speak with the people who we were getting money off and she'd do it in a very calm manner which could only be perceived as speaking civilly. Amanda would tell the people involved that she didn't want me involved so if they gave her £3,000 she'd put the other £2,000 in and you can give me it back when you've got it. Amanda could do it in a way where they'd be thanking her in the end. On one job like that we must have got about £120,000 off him using that exact trick.

I'm telling you now the money in cigarettes is phenomenal. In fact, there's more money to be made selling fags than there is class A drugs and also the prison sentences are nowhere near as high. The reason we got so much from that fag dealer was that I found out he'd been making and selling guns and also his brother-in-law was a copper. In the end, he was posting £20,000s through his front letterbox when we went to his door to keep us quiet.

A lot of people I knew who'd been paid off from British Steel would invest thousands upon thousands into fag runs abroad. At that time in the years I'm talking about in this chapter it was 2008/09 I had money growing out my fucking ears. I was giving my Mam £1,000 every time I saw her as well as my siblings and even Terry Dicko. On an average day I would have maybe sixty people at my house asking to lend money and I'd give it away. I would give kids in the street £20 because they had nothing or their shoes would have holes in I was fucking crackers with money. As quick as the money was flowing in it was going out even faster. It all went Pete Tong in the end because I badly managed everything.

I'll give you an example, say if a security company owed me £600 but it wasn't due for them to pay for another month, I'd send Amanda down to say if you pay £300 now you can keep the other £300 and that's the reason why I lost an empire. Me and Amanda were as bad as each other on drugs so I'm not calling her. We both badly needed help but we didn't think we were as bad as each other but that's what drug addicts do isn't it. It was at that time as well that I had The One Show programme from the BBC approach me asking if they could do a feature episode on my life. In fact, the fella turned up at my door and when he came in I gave him a book and sat him down and he told me that he was relieved I was so approachable as he'd been shitting himself about coming. The presenter told me he couldn't believe how intellectual I was and that he thought he was going to meet some big thick caveman.

Another guy from The Daily Mirror tracked me down called Anton Ivanovich who did a story on me. He offered me all kinds of things but I let that go down the pan also.

It was around 2009 that the beginning of the end started for me and Amanda. I'd been with Amanda since 1996/97 but we were drifting away. We never even slept in the same room for the last two years of our relationship and there was no intimacy. We became more like brother and sister in the end and she walked out on me in 2013. I knew if somebody doesn't love you that you can't make them stay and our relationship was over but I'll come to that later in the book.

"You can fool some of the people all of the time, and all of the people some of the time, but you cannot fool all of the people all of the time."

Abraham Lincoln

CHAPTER 9

MELTING THE ICEMAN

Around 2010/11 I seemed to be doing a lot of jobs debt collecting for the sum of £1000, so whatever these people who hired me were owed we'd go half each 50/50 all the way. I would tell these victims of frauds that 50% in your pocket and 50% in my pocket is better than 100% in their pockets. After I did the job for that person I also gave them a lifetime guarantee that I'd watch their back for repercussions very much like Roy Shaw used to.

How I got mixed up with the notorious Ice Man in Billingham was through me getting a phone call from a well-known villain named Chris Curry. Chris was from Billingham himself and he'd been in and out of jail all his life. I'd had a fight with Chris myself years ago as well as me also being in prison but we became good friends so when Chris rang me and asked if it would be ok to see me, we agreed to meet up. So when me and Chris were talking he told me that there was a lad he knew named Danny who'd done two tours of Iraq which got my respect straight away. Let me tell you now, when people ask me who my heroes are in life I may say George Best, Muhammad Ali or Mike Tyson but really deep down my real hero's in life are the service men and women like this kid Danny. As Chris told me more of the story I became sadder and sadder by the minute. It turns out that this kid Danny had to be medically discharged by the British Army as he'd gone a bit "ga-ga" after seeing his mates blown to bits in front of him. I had tears in my eyes when Chris was now telling me that Danny walks around not knowing what day it is and with his underpants on his head that type of thing. I began to realise the full extent of the real reason Chris had phoned me when he told me that Danny had received an Army pension but he'd lent it to this lad named Alinson and he went on the run with it which I found to be an outright fucking liberty. This one didn't sit well with me and I took it personally because this guy who'd been had over was one of life's true hero's! At the time I was banned from driving I couldn't get over to see this Alinson fella so Chris arranged for me to get a lift over in a really tiny car, you can imagine what this looked like with me in it. In fact the lad who took me was a pizza delivery boy that Chris had organised. Anyway, me and the pizza delivery boy take a drive over to Billingham and we stop off at a pub which was called The Merlin to meet this Danny to get more of the picture. When I spoke to this hero he told me he lent this guy X amount of money which was a large sum by the way. Danny told me he wanted to give me half if I could collect it but I told Danny I don't want a penny for this, this one's personal to me so off I went on the hunt. Now I'm off to the address fucking raging and full of fuck. Whoever has had this true hero of a man over is going to feel the wrath of Big Bri BIG TIME. So, Chris Curry drives me over there and when we get outside the address I noticed there were kids in the street so we parked around the corner out of sight. Even though I was blowing fire I would have accepted it if this Alinson started paying Danny £50 a week but as I was walking to the door I saw the man who was well known as "The Iceman." Well he was the biggest man I've ever seen in the flesh. The guy was 6ft 10 and 26st. I didn't know then but later I learned that this Iceman was well known in Nottingham until he stabbed someone there and got five years in jail and ended up North. The reason The Iceman was there in the first place was he was going out with this Alinson's mam so he was a kind of stepfather to this rip off merchant Alinson. I later found out that Alinson's mam was getting men back from pubs and then this Iceman and her son Alinson were robbing them as well as flooding the streets of Teesside with drugs of the worst fucking kind. This isn't my opinion, the gang who were doing this evil operation ended up getting many years in jail.

This Iceman was so big he'd actually featured on the telly on a Bacardi Breezer advert on a beach. Now I'm not trying to baffle you here but me and Amanda were abroad and on that beach when that advert with The Iceman was filmed 15 years earlier and now I was about to go to war with that very guy. It's fucking insane isn't it?! Anyway, when I came face to face with this Iceman, he was the biggest man I've ever seen. Even when I went to the world's strongest man competitions and met the competitors they were nowhere near this massive fucker. He was like The Mountain from Game of Thrones. As I was walking to meet this total unit I noticed he said something which sounded like "wait a minute" but I couldn't quite hear him because of the kids in the street. The next minute I turn around and I see this Iceman walk over to Chris my friend and hit him over the head with a little samurai sword, Chris's glasses fell off then the Iceman dragged poor Chris in the house. As soon as I saw him drag Chris in the house I ran over to the front door, at the time I weighed only probably about just over 18 stone because of the crack. To be honest I was out of condition but the rage inside me was so strong I had to save my friend. As I looked through the front room window I could see the Iceman and another five of his mates hitting Chris with bats and other evil looking weapons so I screamed, "LEAVE HIM ALONE YOU'RE KILLING HIM" and I kicked the door, as I did that half the wall came through with the door. As soon as Chris saw me he was shouting, "he's my man he's my man" obviously trying to warn them off him as the blows were still raining down on him. When I saw Chris he was a total mess and I think he ended up with twenty three stitches after it as well as all his ribs broken the lot. Chris would have been killed if it wasn't for me. Anyway, I'm now in this crack den (but not by choice this time) and obviously they can all see me now inside so I kick another set of doors open and the gang try to leg it out the back door of the house but I managed to grab hold of the Iceman's neck, turned him around and smacked him as hard as I could which nearly took his fucking head off and he's hit the deck. I was just about to really unload on him when the Iceman's Mrs, jumped on my back and grabbed my arms but at this point the Iceman's shouting, "RING THE POLICE RING THE POLICE." Now you've got this giant bully of a man lying on the floor calling for his girlfriend to call the authorities and all his friends, it was fucking unbelievable. Looking back at it now I feel awful because I was going berserk hitting anyone because there was young children in the house but at the time I didn't think because they were killing my mate. In the end, I've picked what was left of Chris up and put him over my shoulder and got him out in the garden and put him in the car then I went back for revenge. I was stood outside of the house calling the Iceman all sorts and asking him to face me like a man but he wouldn't. He was shouting through the doors in his broad West Indian accent to get away from his house but within seconds I could hear the police helicopters so that was it and I fucked off to the young kid from my documentary Ryan's house with Chris and we stayed there for three days. Amanda was at home when this happened but she rang me and asked what I had done! I said, "what do you mean?" She said, "there's police helicopters hovering above our house." With police helicopters you can hear them even from miles away. After I spoke with Amanda I went back to attending to Chris who by now was in a really bad way. His head was wide open and I told him I'd have to get him to a hospital or he was going to die. In the end, we put this sort of turban on his head and I arranged to get him to the hospital. As soon as I got there I got a call from one of the top Cleveland police inspectors asking me to give him my version of events but I told him to fuck off. I said, "what are you going to do? Nick me for saving someone's life?" I wasn't too happy but he very calmly told me that he needed to see me and that the Iceman and gang have gone to the police wanting to press charges against me. I told him not to insult my fucking intelligence as there were a load of witnesses, I mean we're talking about a hot summer day here with a lot of people in the street who witnessed exactly what happened.

They called this guy "The Iceman" because he'd been involved at a high level in the distribution of crystal meth. What was even more staggering was after all that happened I got the blame for shooting the Iceman's windows through in a drive-by shooting when I was on remand in Holme House by the police. All I can say is I must have long fucking arms to shoot his windows at his home from my prison cell. I know one of the headlines in the papers about it was, "The Iceman Melts When the Taxman Hits Him" not long after it.

A couple of days later I was back at home with Amanda and I thought it must have all blown over so I went to see how Chris was recovering. Chris was staying at Elvis Tomo's on Durham Road in Stockton. When I got there there was a well-known Middlesbrough man that goes by the name of a Nintendo game character! He wasn't in my good books because I had taken him out all weekend and spent a fortune on him, then a few days later I got told he said, "ha Brian's a big daft cunt he took me out all weekend and I must have had two grand off him buying the drugs etc"… I wasn't in the mood for him but I also heard he'd been in my brother's house and he'd stolen a small sum of money. I know it sounds nothing but it was my brother Skinny who'd now died. Anyway, he was there and he was giving it all the big un saying, "I'm not scared of you Cockerill" which was making me boiling but I didn't want to hit him in front of these two prostitutes which were there because they're the biggest grasses walking. Anyway, I noticed he walked down the stairs and he had the audacity to say something else and straight away I've banged him and knocked him into next week. He tried to get up put I pinned him on a bed and said come on then what have you got to say now and I was strangling him to the point of almost death. This guy was a real lowlife and a pure bully who used to tax little kids and prostitutes the lot. I had so much rage in me that I put my finger in his eye and popped it and blood poured out. He then still tried to get up but then I really walloped him three times 'BANG BANG BANG' and that's when I split all his temple wide open and he was crying like a baby saying he loved me but I told him he was nothing but a fucking pure scumbag lowlife bully.

At that time a lot of people in Teesside were saying, "oh he's finished that Brian Cockerill" but I did the Iceman and a well-known Middlesbrough bully in the same week so I can't have been that finished. Even though I was a ravaged crackhead I could still fight for fun with the strength of a seven-foot wild bear. I know first-hand that people used to say, "oh Brian's not the man he was" and maybe that's true but I'd still be too much for most men out there if I wanted to live that life but of course I don't. I wouldn't want that life for all the money in the world. All I want is peace and quiet, to be able to settle down with my Wife, to be able to look after my brother Bobby, walk my dog Scrappy and help people with my experiences of the bad things I've been involved with.

Going back to leaving Elvis Tomo's and seeing Chris was ok and having dusted that Nintendo character well and fucking truly, I went back home and went back on the gear but I wasn't going to be alone. I heard a loud noise outside and it's said, "COME OUT QUIETLY COCKERILL IT'S THE ARMED POLICE" I looked out and it was like the Michael Caine Zulu film when there were fucking loads of the bastards all pointing guns at my house. I thought I've had enough of these fuckers and I went out, bearing in mind I was off my boiler and I'd been on the pipe at the time and I shouted, "I'M SPARTACUS." The armed response must have thought, he's fucking crackers this fella! I ended up getting nicked and locked up and put in the cells.

The police custody suites aren't the nicest places at the best of times but when you're coming down off all the gear you've been on its fucking ten times worse please believe me. When I was in the custody office I was told I was getting done for the attempted murder of 'The Iceman' and aggravated burglary but I wasn't bothered because I hadn't done anything wrong. Yes, I'd smashed Nintendo man to bits but the police didn't know about that and with the Iceman there was a street full of witnesses to back me up on what the truth was. Well just how wrong I was! Even though I told the police the names of the witnesses the police told me they couldn't find any of them and I was put on remand for 110 days in Holme House. The police then told me they couldn't find the lad who's car took me from the pizza shop even though there was only one pizza shop on the road I gave them to go to. Also, Danny the poor Army fella seemed to not be of importance to them even though the guy was a model citizen who'd served his country.

The fact of the matter is that, in my opinion, Cleveland police just wanted to steal 110 days of Brian Cockerill's life which is what they did.

Normally the police's job is to go out and gather all the evidence then present it to the CPS and they make the decision which never happened. Can you imagine if they spoke to eyewitnesses saying that it was the Iceman who hit the guy over the head with a sword and it was Brian who was only saving his mates life! It should have been black and white but the police wanted their pound of flesh with Brian Cockerill.

After I was interviewed for several hours then Cleveland police came back with the attempted murder charge dropped but it was still assault and the aggravated burglary charges and they sent me to Holme House.

When I arrived inside Holme House, word had already got around the full prison that "Cockerill's in" and you'd thought a fucking celebrity had arrived. At one point I was actually laid in my cell and I could hear at the windows in stage whispers, "big Bri's in", "Scotch Bri's arrived" and "The Taxman's in" etc etc blah blah…

When I arrived the screws were knocking on my door asking me to sign books and all sorts. The first day I arrived in prison I was 18st 6lbs and I thought, fucking hell I've lost some fucking weight so I knew I had to rebuild. In a way, I suppose it was a blessing in disguise to keep me away from all the gear I'd been going through. The best thing that happened to me in jail was when a screw came up to me and said, "can I have a word with you big fella?" This lovely prison officer went by the name of Mr Davison and he used to be an ex-boxer from Grangetown. Mr Davison told me that he was putting me on his wing and he was going to see I was alright. Bless Mr Davison he tried to get me a good job in the jail but the governor refused saying that I was too high profile and too much of a risk if I decided to kick off. I really appreciated Mr Davison because he fought my corner and he told the governor that I could control the full prison single handedly. The governor fully understood his point but he also said that if I also clicked my fingers I could have the full jail under my command if I wanted to turn the other way which I fully understood.

When I was in Holme House that time in 2011 obviously I became the daddy of the full prison. In my time there I met Simon Vallily who'd not long before won a Heavyweight Boxing Commonwealth Gold Medal in Delhi only the year before. I used to train with Simon and I talked him out of one or two fights. I tried to nurture him as I found Simon to be a lovely lovely kid but just a bit misunderstood. When Simon was freed and he went on to become pro he phoned me after one of his fights and I was so thrilled for him. His brother Carl is also another one I have a lot of time for but he's been a bit naughty in the past.

After I'd been in prison for a few weeks and settled in I thought fuck it, I'm going to start training again for the first time in well over six months. At first I started with your simple press-ups and sit-ups and after a bit I was eventually allowed in the gym. In fact when I was in the gym at Holme House there was an old screw who'd been there since the last time I was in through the early 90s and he told me he remembered when I did over 700lbs in front squat and it was fucking unbelievable and it was still spoken of for years after I left by the gym screws. My nickname in the jail gym was 'The Ultimate Warrior' because I was in there training like a fucking maniac. The young kids used to gather around me in the gym and they'd say, "his fucking legs are huge" and I'd say, "I wish everything was fucking huge" and they'd laugh their heads off.

If ever I was on the prison association all the young kids would want to be sat next to me wanting me to tell them stories of Lee Duffy, Viv Graham and taxing etc…

On the savoury there used to be a rule which said one man two sausages but I was given what I wanted. One time this really rough looking bird screw said, "give him only one portion" but Mr Davison was the S.O and told her I was more than one man and for the kitchen staff to give me what I wanted.

When I was inside I was the only man in the prison to be allowed to wear my own clothes because now none of the prison issue clothing would fit me. To tell you the truth I didn't mind it in prison because I was allowed to help people. I helped a lot of these young lads out with their paranoia and I sat down and tried to talk some sense into them.

One lad who was in from Darlington, had just lost his dad and I was allowed to spend a bit of time with him and help him grieve.

Please don't think I'm being in anyway big headed when I say this but I was viewed in prison by the whole system as some kind of fucking god! At times I'd be sat on association and out of the sixty, they'd be forty listening to me giving out advice. I would stand there above all these young impressionable kids who would look up to me as if I was their schoolteacher all asking the same questions, "what was it like being punched by Lee Duffy?" and "what was it like fighting with Dave Garside?" I would tell them, that they didn't have to keep on doing the same stupid shit and ruining their lives. Even the screws would sit and listen and they'd tell me I had a gift for talking (just ask Jamie Boyle).

One incident I remember was when some lad got his trainers stolen, I stood up on association and said, "listen I don't care who's got them just make sure them trainers are back within the hour or I'll be coming round all your fucking pads!" I told them all that we're all in the same boat and if anyone hasn't got anything then to come and see me and I'll try sort something. Within twenty minutes those Nike Air Max were back anonymously.

Another well-known boxer from Teesside who was in there at the time was former pro Mark Owens. I was with Mark when I did 850kg leg press with eleven reps. All the screws witnessed that and it's still on the wall in the prison today along with Mark Davison and Bud Armstrong from Newcastle. People were shouting, "BRIAN FOR FUCKS SAKE" and saying my legs were like a carthorse's.

Going back to Mark Owens he asked me to sign his leg when I got out and he went to get my signature tattooed on his leg.

One of my friends Ali Johnson used to say I wasn't from this planet and that I had the strength of an alien. Ali was in great shape as well so I took that as a massive compliment. I used to train with Ali from the age of 20 to 26 and he used to squat with me. When Ali used to train with me I used to kill him and send him home to bed for the day (laughs).

When I was in prison for the Iceman my pad used to be like Sainsbury's and sometimes the screws would complain because you're only allowed to have so much. I would often give a lot of it away to the lads who never had anything.

What I'd like to state is that I never ever did what Lee Duffy did by going and taking things off them. Many times I also showed these kids how to train and how to eat properly.

After the first few weeks when I got my head around prison I came to the conclusion in life that being in there was part of my tax that I had to pay back to God. Even though I was innocent this time I'd done a lot of other bad things which I'd never been caught for so it was my karma wasn't it!

Looking back today in 2020, that prison sentence saved me from killing myself with the crack cocaine. It was my wake-up call and a break from what wasn't reality.

When I first arrived at 18st 6lbs I could hardly do more than two press-ups because I was that weak. When I left I was able to do over a hundred everyday as well as sit-ups. A lot of the time I'd be shadow boxing in my cell and I'd have Sky News on which had a clock in the corner so I could time 3-minute rounds. When I was doing that sometimes the adverts would come on and the clock would go off and I'd be like, 'OOH FOR FUCKS SAKE' because it would ruin my whole workout and I'd punch walls. Many times I would look out the window and the full landing opposite would have the lights out and I'd think, what's going on! Then I realised that everybody was watching me shadow box.

At the end of that sentence I would pray to God and I'd pray to my brother Peter, I'd say if you're watching Skinny I could do with a hand here kid and he must have heard me because I got a letter from my barrister whose name was Peter Makepeace, I'll never forget it. What's more bizarre was the prosecutors name was Peter as well and the Judge's, it was crazy. It wasn't just my little brother sending help from above because my old buddy Chris Curry then tried to prosecute the Iceman because he received horrific injuries in the attack. Luckily Amanda and Jordan went to one of the neighbours to come forward to tell the truth which he took to the police even though they didn't want it. Overall the whole event of me saving my friends life was watched by two women and four men but not one was interviewed by Cleveland police. All the police were interested in was putting away that Brian Cockerill who usually turned up kicking doors down and started going radio rental (Glasgow slang for fucking mental). What also fucked the police was a thing called undisclosed. Unbeknown to me at the time it turns out some old dear saw what went on and phoned 999 which was all recorded and it was played. She said that a great big black man has just hit a man over the head with a weapon and that his glasses had fallen off. Then she was heard to say, "hang on a minute, there's a big white man just come and he's trying to save his mates life." She also went on to say that I first shouted, "get off your killing him" and banged on the windows. It was played out like a football matches commentary on Match of the Day and she was saying just how much blood Chris lost (three pints of blood the hospital said). Now bearing in mind I'd just spent 110 days in prison it turns out that another two 999 calls were made by an old man saying that I dragged my mate out and now it looks like him and the black lad were going to fight. It turns out that I lost three and a half months of my life for nothing and everything I told the police was true!

Well, in the end it didn't even make the proper courts because I got a phone call telling me I was now free to walk! In fact, the judge who was reviewing the case said I didn't belong in prison but I should have been given a medal of bravery for saving my friends life. I was told at the end of this horrible unfair process that the police had told the courts that Mr Cockerill was known for firearms and even though they'd arrested me for aggravated burglary, apparently I told some officers I was coming back to shoot them so I needed to be kept off the streets. When I had my chance to answer that in court I stood up and I said, "can I just stop you there please?" I then asked, "where does it say on my record that I've been involved with firearms?" Then I said, "that's right it doesn't so are we dealing in a world of fantasy here or proven facts?" One of the officers even said they knew all about what Brian Cockerill gets up to but then I simply stated, "I could call you a paedophile, rapist or a thief but I've got no proof so because you're saying you think you know what I'm like I've had to lose a big chunk of my life for nothing?!" I asked again where was the proof and the judge said that I was right. I told them all that all I wanted to do was stand in front of a Crown Court judge because those magistrates were a waste of time. I said you're all shopkeepers, bank managers and Lidl staff and you know nothing about the law. I said all you're doing is listening to the clerks of this court. At one-point Chris Curry stood up crying telling them all that I had done was save his life. Chris told the magistrates that he wouldn't be here today and that they would have been dealing with a murder case if it wasn't for Brian Cockerill.

Going back to the Iceman himself and the reason I was in prison in the first place. When I got there I had a screw coming to shake my hand and when I asked him what for he said, "that Iceman piece of shit had my daughter on the crack and tried to get her on the game so you want a fucking medal for doing what you did." I was told the big coward got moved away not long after but I heard he also reported another two people and had them arrested for similar incidents the big cowardly bastard. Another screw also thanked me for getting him out of Billingham. He told me off the cuff that a lot of prison officers in Holme House thought the world of me for what I had done and at times for free.

You know sometimes I would tell all the kids in the jail not to pick on the screws and that they were only doing their jobs. Then again there was this horrible screw like that little fucker from The Green Mile named Porteous and I went right up to his face and screamed, "I'LL FUCKING KILL YA" just for the craic and he went white. It must have been like a wild untamed lion roaring in his face but Mr Davison was laughing because he knew I had a point. I told everybody on the wing to never ask Mr Porteous for fuck all because he'll always say no just to be spiteful. I used to say, "go ask Mr Davison because he's a fair man and if its legally right he'll say yes." Mr Davison knew this Porteous was a total arsehole but he couldn't say anything because he was a fellow colleague. If you're reading this Mr Davison you always were a proper gent and a total professional at your job.

Another thing I did in prison was when I saw two lads fighting so I ran up to them and roared, "FUCKING BREAK IT UP NOW" and both lads went white and stopped throwing blows. Then I turned to the screws who were watching and I said, "if I break this up now they're both not going to get nicked are they?" And the screws assured me both wouldn't, so then I went "you get to your cell and you fucking move as well" and both ran. After I did that I had a few screws coming to my cell telling me thanks for what I did earlier. Just before I left the prison a few of the officers told me I'd been brilliant and in all the time I'd been in there was no bother at all in the whole prison. Mr Davison said something different, he said, "I wanted you to get ten years Cockerill because the whole jails fucking brilliant with you in here and I actually looked forward to coming to work." At the end of it all a few of them told me that before I was coming in they'd all heard of my fearsome reputation but they only found me to be polite. Many said I was nothing like what was in Steve Richards' book or the Donal Macintyre documentary. Another woman I'd like to give a special mention to was Fliss Watson who helped me writing letters because I can't write for two reasons, one because I'm dyslexic and two my hands are all knackered from the weights and fighting. I'm a fantastic reader and my IQ is 134 but I struggle with admin work so Fliss was a real hero to me when I was inside. Although I wasn't brilliant at writing I did NVQ's in Maths and English which was a three-week course but I passed it within three days.

Going back to when this Iceman incident got flung out I'll never forget when one of the barristers said, "this Cockerill fella has done nothing wrong and its Cleveland police who are at wrong here." He then said that Cleveland police should have done their job thoroughly but it's clear as day that they haven't. Looking back I should have sued them and without a doubt, I'd have made a lot of money because in a lot of professional people's eyes it was malicious towards me. What really finished it for the case going to Crown Court was the CPS telling the police that it was impossible to take this man to court because it's impossible to get a conviction with the factual evidence that was presented. Also that Brian Cockerill doesn't even know the three people who called 999 at that precise time so why would those elderly people go on to make statements at a later date?

What pissed me off most of all was some of the witnesses next door to where it happened told Amanda that some of the evidence was hidden by the Iceman and his gang. Stuff like a rounders bat full of Chris Curry's blood and the samurai sword. This neighbour told Amanda that she knew the Iceman hid all those things but she was frightened to make a statement to the police because she still had to live next door to them. After Amanda spoke to the neighbours well after the Iceman and co were removed they then rang the police and told them they had all the stuff that they'd been made to hide which had Chris Curry's blood and DNA all over but they were told that they were no longer needed and the case is going ahead, that would have saved me and Chris Curry 110 days in prison on its own. That's fucking outrageous isn't it but I have all the factual statements in my home to this day. My barrister told me, "Brian this is pure corruption at the highest level."

I know a lot of you will be reading this thinking well if all this is true then why didn't I sue them but the truth of it was I was a pathetic crackhead. I was smart enough upstairs to do things like that and get the ball moving but when the only thing in your life that matters is smoking crack everything else is out the window. If that had happened to the Brian Cockerill of today I'd have sued them to fuck. I did actually speak with a barrister who knew an awful lot about the case and he told me how foolish I was because I'd have got a hell of a lot of money. When you look at my friend the old solicitor Jimmy Watson who got arrested and put through hell he got almost half a million so what would I have got? I know Jimmy Watson very well and he was the best in the business at what he did. Him and Nick Woodhouse were even going to vote for me for mayor.

When other people were saying I couldn't have been mayor because I was a career criminal I would tell them that Ray Mallon has got more convictions than me and he was the chief of police.

If any of you Cleveland police who were involved with putting an innocent man away I'd like to thank you all from the bottom of my heart. You put me on an all-inclusive holiday at her royal highness' pleasure and got me off the crack. When I came out I was back to 21 stone and looked a picture of health although I was white as a sheet but a few sunbed sessions sorted that.

One of the things that was nice and helped me to cope with what I'd been through was what the judge told me at the end of it. He said, "I'm sorry Mr Cockerill that you had to spend 110 days in jail because of this." He said, "in my opinion you should have been given a medal and not a prison sentence because what you did was pure bravery. All I can do now is apologise and I'd like to speak to Cleveland police myself and I'm going to look into this."

I did hear that that big pathetic piece of shit The Iceman went around after our fight telling people how he knocked The Taxman out and broke my jaw blah blah blah blah but there must have been around over one thousand people who saw me in Holme House not long after without a mark on me. Most nights in Holme House we'd often talk out of the windows at night. Mainly I'd chat to Mark Davison and Chris Curry. Anybody who knows me knows I can talk forever so I'd be ranting all night keeping people awake. Sometimes voices would pop up saying, "Brian we're getting a bit tired here" but I'd tell them to get to bed and stop being fucking nosey. Often people would shout out, "WHO THE FUCK KEEPS TALKING?" And I'd say, "it's me Brian Cockerill" and then they'd usually say, "aah it is ok then mate carry on." Often I would be at the window giving people legal advice like I was their barrister.

When I would be up at the windows most nights I would always be singing Johnny Cash's 'Burning Ring of Fire' because I like all the old songs and that is my favourite. When I got out of prison there was a lovely girl named Yvette Wood who even got some 'The Taxman' t-Shirts printed of me and many people walked around and wore them in my support. Thank you Yvette X.

"Live your own life because you die your own death".

Brian Cockerill

CHAPTER 10

DEEP AND CONTROVERSIAL

Now this might be controversial but in my opinion I think they should legalise heroin in Teesside.

Before people think I've gone crackers listen to my reasons. How many people are dying of overdoses? If an addict has to go and steal for £20 worth they'll go burgle someone's house and straight away you've got a locksmith who has to repair that window. Then the police, insurance companies, probation are involved and they'll then catch the culprit who then gets arrested. That person arrested now needs a solicitor and he has to go right through the courts i.e. needing a judge, barrister, court clerk etc etc... Then when they arrive in prison it costs £500 per day to look after that burglar. By the time that person has been right the way through all the systems its cost £20,000 plus.

If they were given legalised heroin it would cost about £2 - £10 to administrate the drug and if that was happening then people wouldn't be burgling houses because they'd be getting heroin for nothing. That would stomp out all the gangsters selling heroin.

The flipside is, and this is better than anything, is that the Taliban who make 90% of their income from smack wouldn't receive this anymore because if you aren't aware that filth comes from Afghanistan and Pakistan and it gets shipped to England. If you cut that supply then the Taliban wouldn't have the riches to buy all the dangerous weapons they do which would stop the terrorism. Just think how much of that money could then go to hospitals, schools and more police forces. Can you think of how much the prison system would benefit from this, it would certainly take the pressure off the overcrowding issue.

Why would you go burgle a house for smack when you can now get it for free? If these addicts were given a certain amount nobody would be overdosing! Today we have enough zombies out there and it's only going to get worse. If someone's going to take drugs then you won't be able to stop them from taking it if they're addicted. People out there aren't going to think, I'm going to go on heroin because it's free! The only ones who are going to take that stuff are the people who are already ravaged by the poison in the first place. In fact, it was only in the tabloids on September 15th, 2019 if you Google it, they were saying that they were considering doing exactly what this chapter is suggesting.

Many years ago when I was in Thorpe Arch prison in 1996 in Yorkshire I had what you might call an epiphany and I was talking around a table at a meeting in jail saying just this. The governor and lots of officers were all there listening to what I was coming out with. If this does happen the British government would save billions of pounds over the years and not to mention that the crime rates would go down.

Listen, although I've never been convicted for a great deal apart from driving offences, I've been inside prison on remand a few times, although I didn't get a conviction. I know all of those people inside the jails, I'd say over 80% were there because they were on drugs and its mostly heroin.

All the other drugs are recreational because it's only psychological. When you're on heroin you need it like you need food and water. Now Cleveland police have become vocal and are seemingly backing this idea which has even been in The Gazette and I just pray to god something becomes of it.

Another funny tale which is similar, is the well know Middlesbrough clairvoyant Gary Fowler told me around the millennium that at some point in the future I was going to do great things with the drug problems in Teesside. I was never really into the hocus pocus bullshit people but a friend of mine Kevin Kilty asked me if I'd see Gary. As I was 100% sceptical, I only met Gary for Kevin's sake. When I eventually met Gary Fowler, who turned out to be a lovely guy by the way, I was so glad I met him. Gary told me that he had a message for me but before he began he said, "forewarned is forearmed" which means if you've been warned you're going to be ready for it. Gary went on to tell me that I needed to be extremely vigilant with people with knives. Gary told me that he felt that somebody was going to try and stab me which actually did go on to happen several times and I've always dealt with it. Gary also told me that he had a message from Lee Duffy. Gary went on to say that Lee told me that he loved me and that he was doing ok and he's at peace. Now I'm the biggest non-believer in stuff like that so when Gary told me things that only Lee would have known I was blown away. Gary said that Lee was telling him to tell me he loved me like a brother and that I had to calm down and live my life. After Gary stopped giving me messages from The Duffer he started going in another completely different direction. Gary all of a sudden came out with, "the only way Cleveland police win their war with narcotics is by coming to people like you Brian." Then he also added, "you might think I'm talking rubbish here Brian but in many years from now, Middlesbrough council and the police are going to ask you to go around schools and help these people." Gary told me that he could feel a massive aura coming off me which was only positive. Gary told me that I had a purple energy coming off me and it's only a matter of time before the authorities would get in touch which they have whilst I've been doing this book with Jamie Boyle.

I think everything happens for a reason and although my first book with Steve Richards' happened, doing this with Jamie I believe was made by the Gods from above. I believe that it was fate that Jamie got in touch with me so he could give me a media platform so I could carry out my good deeds.

Gary Fowler came to see me again at my house at a later date and again came out with some more stuff that blew me away. Gary asked how my new girlfriend was, well I hadn't even told him that I had a new girlfriend. In fact, at this precise time, I'd only went on one date with this lass and never told a soul not even my brother Bobby. One of the things that Gary told me that day has always stayed with me, he said, "Brian when you're sucking that pipe it's the devil that's getting in you and that's what's making you ill". Gary told me he loved me because I was a really good person. Gary said that I had so much potential in me but I was ruining it all with the drugs. He told me that I could help so many people in this world that it's unbelievable and that the reason I hadn't been killed like Lee Duffy, Viv Graham and Peter Hoe was God had kept me here for a purpose but I just didn't realise it yet! I very shamefully didn't listen to him and I continued to take drugs for many years until I met up with Jamie Boyle.

If you're reading this Gary Fowler thank you so much for your input and it may have taken me many years but I now know what you were trying to tell me. Gary Fowler did come to see me only last year and he told me again that he was worried about me and that he knew I'd been calling him and I had. Gary told me there and then that day that I needed to get off the gear and that it was wiping me out and destroying my brain. Gary pleaded with me to trust in God, himself and beat this shit once and for all, he told me if I needed him day or night that I had his number but at that point I was still too ill and weak to make a change. It was only this book that has helped me rebuild my life.

"There's an old saying which goes, you run from a knife and charge at a gun because you can't outrun a bullet."

Brian Cockerill

CHAPTER 11

JUST ANOTHER MURDER ACCUSATION

In 2011 there was a murder in Teesside and it ended up that I was linked to it in the most comical way. What happened was a couple of lads decided to kidnap some poor guy and one of the texts sent to the victim beforehand was that Brian Cockerill was involved. So, when the guys got arrested and they checked the phones they saw my name on one of the texts. The reality is I'd never even met any of the people involved in the murder. Not long after the murder I get a call from the murder squad. I was in the house minding my own business when the top squad at Cleveland police came to the door. I opened the door and funny enough it was the same weekend that Osama bin Laden was killed so I told them, "if it's for that murder I will own up to that because I want the 250 million reward for doing him in." I said to them "that's one murder I will admit to." Jokes aside it was down to a few lads named Lee Woodier, George Thomas Jnr, his son Stephen Thomas and a guy named Andrew Jackson. All but Woodier were given a minimum of twenty years a piece, Woodier got five years for manslaughter plus five more for the kidnapping. I was dragged into it because one of the fuckers that killed poor John Newton used my name. Well I was asked if I knew about John Newton being murdered and I told them of course I did and it was sad. I read that John Newton's wife had a baby girl the next day which is fucking terrible that had happened to her. The police were asking what I knew about it but I think it dawned on them that I knew fuck all but then they asked me to make a statement and it was a chance to get them back. I told them I don't make statements to the police no matter what.

The tragic thing is that poor guy John Newton was taken in a van and beaten to death and even my friend David Woodier got dragged into it but he hadn't done anything like me. That is just another blatant example of my name being dragged into things on Teesside when I haven't done anything at all that was linked with that murder. All it was was the last text on his phone was someone telling this poor guy who got murdered that Brian Cockerill was now involved.

Again the police were telling me to make a statement but it was never going to happen. Brian Cockerill doesn't make statements to the police. In fact, when I was fighting Dave Garside, Dave Woodier was the only one to step in and help me when Garside was getting the better of me. From that day forward David Woodier was my friend for life. He's my pal.

I told the murder squad "I'm extremely sorry that this poor man has been murdered but it's really nothing to do with me." The police went away and left me alone but I was told my name was read out in court.

That wasn't the only murder I was linked to, back in the summer of 2003 I was a suspect and they came to my house. At that time I was really bad on the crack and suffering from paranoia so it didn't help when the murder squad put a note through my door saying they wanted to talk to me about the murder of Dougie Manders. To cut a long story short I went down to the old Middlesbrough police station on Dunning Road. When I went in I was told to sit down by the top officers, then they went on to tell me that they'd been told that me and BJ Crossling were supposed to have kidnapped him, beat him up then put him in some container with a load of logs on top of him. I knew they were just putting it on me to see if I'd give them information. I told them I knew exactly what they were doing and they were just fishing. Well they were fishing with the wrong man. I told them I couldn't tell them fuck all and that was that.

Back in 1996 Mark Sayers was shot and killed in Redcar and the police linked me to that also even though I was in jail.

Middlesbrough police have me down as some figure of pure evil who's behind every murder in Teesside. They have me down like Al Capone was in the 1930s in Chicago. If anything happens in Teesside of any huge magnitude then Cockerill must be pulling the strings in the eyes of Cleveland police.

When Mark Sayers was shot he was just taking his dog for a walk when a couple of assailants came along and shot him and even killed his poor dog. Cleveland police thought I was behind the killing of the ex-Grangetown boxer. That was at the same time as when I went away for thirty months for dangerous driving. One thing in court I'll never forget is when the judge said to me, "Mr Cockerill I'm astounded that you've never been to jail before." My reply to that was, "how can you be astounded when there's no evidence!" All I've ever been done for is criminal damage to police cars, shouting at somebody in the street and driving offences it hardly makes me Jack the Ripper! I told judge Scott "the only reason you're astounded is that somebody's told you about me before this court." I said, "you don't know me and I don't know you so how can you be astounded?!" The judge told me to sit down but I told him I wouldn't sit down and I never did. My solicitor told me afterwards that I had some balls because that Judge Scott was notorious for dishing out huge sentences for fun. Judge Scott told me he had his views about me and that was he didn't like me one bit but really a judge shouldn't be allowed to say that. In the end the inevitable happened and that judge remanded me for six fucking months for a driving offence. Judge Scott told me he was going away to America and that when he came back he was going to give me a long sentence so it was personal. When I went to jail all the screws couldn't believe what I was in for. Then when I got sentenced I got thirty months for fucking failing to stop. Nobody got hurt but it wasn't the police that were chasing me it was the armed response because I could drive for fun like a rally driver just like Craig Howard. Craig was the best getaway driver I've ever seen. Some days I was getting chased by the law every single day but my car did 170mph.

Going back to the Mark Sayers murder the reason I was linked with that was because the police heard that he'd been going around saying, "Brian Cockerill's getting out soon and if he comes anywhere near me I'm going to shoot him." Mark Sayers was telling anyone who'd listen that he had some bullets with my name on them. Also Mark Sayers had been in the blues parties looking for me with a gun because they thought I was out. Well I heard about him hunting for me and I thought, you cheeky cunt! I was hearing this from in jail and I was boiling. I knew he lived in Grangetown and as soon as I got out my plan was to go and pay him a visit but I didn't need to. Before I got out two guys paid him a visit in Dormanstown and snuffed his life out. Two men went on to get life sentences for it but the police came to me and said I'd given the go ahead to get him shot which was utterly ludicrous. The police think that Brian Cockerill's the godfather of Middlesbrough and when people come to see me they kiss my hand they bend the knee and all that kind of shit. I think the biggest thing that made them think I was behind the killing was a little dangerous fella named Chino came to see me on the Friday then Mark Sayers was shot on the Saturday. I don't even know how the police got to know that but I'm guessing I was Middlesbrough police's No.1 target, Bambam was No.2 and Speedy was No.3. At that time the regional crime squad and every top police force in the area wanted my head on a plate. Every fucking enforcement unit in the world wanted to take Brian Cockerill down at any cost.

One day I saw a police car in Roseworth, I was going to see my girlfriend and I was with Elvis Tomo and I see this young police officer sneakily talking in some kind of a radio. Now this really annoyed me so I walked over and I asked her "why have you just been talking into that radio about me?" She told me that wherever I was seen they had to radio in so its logged. She told me that the shootings I'd allegedly done I'd always had an alibi for so all the police force logged it when they saw me. That just shows that Cleveland police wanted me so bad it was unbelievable.

Going back to the murder of Mark Sayers the police came to interview me but I told them to fuck off and I had nothing to say to them. I was released a week later and they never bothered coming to see me again because they know Brian Cockerill doesn't talk to the police. The only time I would make a statement was if it was against a paedophile or something really bad to do with kids.

Another murder I was questioned about was when I worked at Philmores in Saltburn. It was owned by a Pakistani guy and it was a rave club. Well there was a guy from Luton in there and he was shot so the cops came from

Luton to interview me. Craig Bier the solicitor (God rest him) told me they wanted to interview me but I told them to fuck right off.

There was big talk in Teesside that I had Speedy (Mark Hornsby) killed. The big fella from Leeds, Clifton Bryan was shot and there was all talk I was behind that. There was also talk I was behind a lad in Billingham being shot but the culprit received twenty years but as soon as that happened I was the first one the police came to see.

When I was on the gear I'd often sit there and I'd be thinking, what if I get nicked for a murder I hadn't even done because I've been arrested for several. That was always a big fear when I was taking stuff. When I'm not on drugs like I'm not today I'm as sharp as a razor and alert and anyone who's been in my company will know. I'm not blowing my own trumpet here but my IQ is 134 and my intelligence is through the roof. I don't think I've got it off anyone I suppose I've just self studied. I've researched on the internet. I'm the type of guy that if you put me on a quiz like The Chase on the telly I'd get 90% of the questions right.

The real Brian Cockerill is so far removed from how I was portrayed on Macintyre's Underworld. Donal even told me he could tell I was highly intelligent but they didn't show that side. What you've got to remember is although that documentary was for one hour I was filmed for over 23 hours. So really they showed the worst hour. In reality if they showed the other true side of me being nice and helping people It wouldn't have made good television viewing. They only wanted to show the monster of Teesside.

I have to thank Donal though for the kindness he showed me when my brother Skinny died, he invited me to stay with him if I wanted to get away from it all for a few days.

A lot of people have used my name in Teesside for extremely naughty things, I mean I've heard people coming up to me saying, "Oh Brian that heroin your selling is bang on," but the truth is I've never fucking sold smack in my life I absolutely despise the filth. One day, I think I told you earlier, I poured over £3,000 of it down the toilet. I fucking hate heroin dealers with a passion and it was always a pleasure taxing them out of all the drug dealers.

A friend of mine used to say to me, "Brian you need to start carrying a gun" but that was never me. All I used to do was slap them and make their ears buzz for a couple of weeks.

Now if you remember Ryan from the Macintyre documentary, he became like a son to me, he even called me dad. Well one day I had to take him to the police station because he'd shot a snowball at somebody. Well unbeknown to us, a local lad had been shot on Redcar Road in Thornaby called Ditty who I didn't know and certainly wasn't involved in it in anyway. I took Ryan to the police station for throwing the snowball and he got a slap on the wrist. On the way home I was planning on dropping Ryan at his girlfriends and me and Amanda were going to get a Chinese when all of a sudden I saw the police following me well I thought shit, my learner plates had fallen off recently due to 100mph winds and I'd already been done before for it so I thought here we go again. Then I saw the armed response coming along and all of a sudden I heard 'NEE NOR NEE NOR NEE NOR NEE NOR' and then four cars came out of nowhere. As I was driving, these police cars were trying to ram me off the road and I thought, I'LL

SMASH YOUR FUCKING FACE IN YA CUNT! I was fucking fuming because I had Ryan, Amanda and Charlie my dog in the car. Then next thing I heard was, "THIS IS THE ARMED POLICE" so they told me to pull over. I knew straight away it wasn't the armed police it was the SAS and they was eight of them. When I pulled over a man of maybe 12st ran over and pointed a gun at me through the car window and told me to sit still and be quiet. As he was telling me this he was looking through the gun spy hole but it was literally about one foot away from me and he was still shouting for me to sit still and shut up. Well I was getting well pissed off so I asked him "why are you looking through your gun target? You can't miss from there surely you fucking idiot!" Then he told me to put my hands up in the air but I was asking him why the fuck was he still looking through his spyhole but all I got back was, "just you stay still Cockerill or I'll blow your fucking head off" but I was telling him all the time he can't be much fucking good if he had to keep looking through that spyhole the fucking nob. Well you wouldn't believe this but I had my hands up for 40 minutes and I've got arthritis in my right hand from the day I fought Lee Duffy while my finger was broken. So I turned around and told G.I. Joe I was getting fucking sick of this so I put my hands down and now G.I. Joe was screaming, "get your fucking hands up Cockerill you're going for a gun and I'll fucking shoot you!" Well by then I was fucking past caring so I told him to shoot me and put me out of my fucking misery. I told this guy he was doing my fucking head in shouting and balling well I can fucking shout and ball and I started screaming at him. I told him "my Mam shouts ten times louder than you ya fucking little rat now fuck off" and I pushed him on the chest and he went flying backwards. Then I got up out of the car and the other officers were pointing all sorts of weapons at me and telling me they'd taser me. Anyway because they were there that long The Evening Gazette had arrived and started taking pictures. If you google Redcar Road Thornaby arrest you can read the full story.

The only reason I was tortured by the armed response was I was just in the area of a shooting at the wrong time and somebody said, "oh there's Brian Cockerill and put two and two together and came up with twenty-two."

What really happened was someone was shot in Thornaby, like three hours before and I happened to be driving past the area with my dog, wife and Ryan. As if I'd have gone to shoot somebody with my dog in the car. If I'd have shot someone I'd have been in fucking Manchester with the Noonans or I'd have been put in a hotel by the Sayers in Newcastle. I know there's a saying which says, the murderer always returns to the scene of the crime but trust me I wouldn't have! Why would I go out and do bad things with the people I love in the car? I wouldn't put their lives at risk.

Anyway going back to the arseholes with the guns pointing at us I shouted, "YOU HURT MY WIFE AND I'LL FUCKING BURY THE LOT OF YOU." I told them that they better shoot me with a rocket launcher, I was fucking blowing fire. There must have been around twelve men stood around my car and I was shouting at them telling them that they're all shithouses. I told them all "get the best fighter out of all of you come to my house and I'll fucking bury you." I said that if they were the SAS then I've seen harder men who work for SCS. My mate Robert Suggett who works for SCS is harder than the lot of them. I was screaming at that them fucking really blowing fire and they were standing back behind their guns but still trying to concentrate on this huge gorilla-type figure who'd just totally lost it. After around fifty minutes the big top police chiefs came and they took Amanda out first but I told the lot of them, I said, "if you touch one hair on her head I'll fucking bury the lot of you." I said, "I'll come for you with everything I've got." I told them I knew they were based in Morpeth but they were telling me to calm down. I told them "how can you expect me to calm down when you've threatened me and my family with guns?!"

In the end they nicked us all but young Ryan was funny because he didn't have a clue what it was about so he said, "this is a bit much for throwing a snowball dad."

When I was talking to my pal Bronson Tyers he told me, "if it wasn't for all those people turning up watching they'd have shot you Brian."

Then one of the big cheeses from the police came and said, "Brian you're under arrest for the shooting earlier on" but I was thinking 'what fucking shooting?' I went on to ask one of the officers why were we waiting so long but he told me when a group get arrested for murder then all the suspects get taken to different police stations. Amanda went to Redcar, Ryan went to Stockton, Charlie my dog went to Middlesbrough and I went to Hartlepool. Another thing before I left was that one of the pricks with the guns said, "if that dog bites me I'll fucking shoot it." Well they couldn't have said anything worse to Brian Cockerill. It was like a red flag to a bull because I fucking loved that dog more than life so I told him when I pointed at him, I said, "I'LL SMASH YOUR FUCKING SKULL IN AND KILL YA STONE DEAD YA BASTARD!" My old dog Charlie, who was on the Macintyre documentary was so vicious because he was sick of getting stopped by police. You only had to see how vicious he was when you watched Macintyre's

Underworld, the dog was only loving to me, Amanda, Jordan and Ryan so anybody after that he was suspicious of. He was crazy when I'd be on the crack he'd be in the other room but he'd stick his nose under the door as if he liked the smell, then the other dog who was a puppy then Scrappy would stick his nose and have a sniff. I used to laugh and think, fucking hell now my dogs are wanting to get on the crack!

Anyway going back to getting locked up for this murder I was put in a van and taken to Hartlepool and I'm in the back thinking that I'm going to get twenty years for something I haven't done. When I got to the police station I knew one of the lads who was working there as I used to train in the gym with him. He wasn't a copper but Group4 and I asked him to loosen the handcuffs because they were hurting my hands. As I was saying that this horrible woman copper said, "don't you dare move" and with that I turned and screamed, "YOU SHUT YA FUCKING MOUTH YOU!" It really must have scared the shit out of her well and truly but the bitch deserved it.

Now I was really on the ball and I told the police that I wanted a DNA expert, fingerprint expert and a powder residue expert all here now. I was bawling that I wanted a forensic officer there to check my clothes which I'd had on all day. By this point I was really thinking I was being set up for a murder. In the end I was put in the cells but they couldn't find any clothes to fit me so they had to go to my house and get some other clothes. Obviously they wanted the clothes I had on for gun residue and DNA matches.

When I was in the cells I was approached by a doctor, which was odd, as in all the dozens of times I've been arrested before this had never happened. Anyway the doctor lifted my top up and he examined me but little did I know at that time that whoever had done the shooting had been stabbed under the armpit. After I was examined by the first doctor another doctor came in and I thought what the fucks going on!

While I was in there, for some reason, they gave me a diazepam which was probably an effort to calm me down. I didn't know this at the time but the police were examining my car and they found a bit of blood which they got very excited over as they were shouting "get in there, we've got him" when really it was my dog Charlie's blood. One of the horrible bastards had hit Charlie in the mouth and knocked one of his teeth out. Well their joy was short-lived because when the tests came back it was canine blood they were fucked on every avenue and were just desperate to put me away. My wife Amanda was marvellous and I mean fucking marvellous she never said a word because I taught her well. In fact the bastards wouldn't let her go to the toilet so she pissed all over the cell floor and shouted to them, "there's my fucking DNA if you want it." They even questioned Amanda telling her "you'll never see your son again, you'll never see your mam again and Brian's going away for a long time" etc etc blah blah blah… In total me, Amanda and Ryan were in there 24 hours but Charlie got out after only three hours which made me think, hang on a minute Charlies fucking grassed me up. The dirty low-life dog bastard has done a deal for two bones and a bit of chicken. I'd had that dog since a pup and he's only gone and blew me up. My best friend Ozzie Bingham went and picked Charlie up for me thank god.

When I was in the cells the police were in my house for twenty hours and they took everything i.e. all my DVD's, ate all my biscuits and drank all the milk that was in the fridge for cups of coffee the cheeky cunts.

I didn't even know the person who was shot so when I was getting questioned they were saying stuff like, "by you're tanned Brian" but I was saying, "what's this got to do with a murder investigation!?" I asked, "whoever has done this was he tanned, 6ft3 and 22stone?" Even when one of the neighbours at the scene told the police, "it wasn't Brian Cockerill I know him because he goes out with my cousin Amanda."

The police came back and a few witnesses saw the shooting that had been carried out by these two men. Suspect one was 5ft 7, medium build, black hair with possible moustache. The other guy I was told had a bald head with ginger freckles! Well how the fuck does that sound like me I ask??? I told the police that they might as well get the Guess Who game in and ask, does he have a beard? Does he wear glasses? Is it Uncle Bob? Does he have a twitch because if he does its Terry Dicko! I've told people since, and even good solicitors have told me, "Brian how the fuck did you get arrested and put through hell for that?!" Then they were telling me the police must have jumped the gun and took the piss out of me!

Going back to when I was in the cells I had one officer walk in and say to me, "Brian I've got some bad news the lad you shot has died and now you're getting done for murder." By then I had a knot in my stomach and I thought you dirty bastards I'm getting lifed off for something I haven't done. I was then transferred to Middlesbrough police station but by then I'd started to kick off. I was thinking, if I'm going to go down for twenty years I'm going to take some of you fuckers with me. I was planning on really fucking some police officers up. I knew that before they could get me on that floor I'd have went mental and broke five of the fuckers jaws. I knew my strength nobody could handle me.

When I got to Middlesbrough police station there was eleven of the biggest and strongest police officers in the force in riot gear. One of the officers told me afterwards he said never ever has there been that many officers on standby for one man. In fact the same officer told me they were really worried when I was about to be brought into custody. When I was in the interview room and they were saying this happened and that happened then you shot him blah blah and I just shook my head. I just told them I was with Terry Dicko so go and ask him. In fact I went to Tesco at the time of the murder so go see them and you'll see me on the cameras.

One of the coppers was called Shane and he was a nice guy and he even said he didn't think I'd killed this person who had been killed. Then he asked me that if I didn't do it then I must know who had done it because Brian Cockerill knows everything in the area according to this officer. I was very respectful to Shane but I told him even if I knew I couldn't do that.

All it really was was there was a murder and I happened to be in the area and they've thought, oh there's Brian Cockerill lets jump the gun (pardon the pun). Well in the end I told the police I was looking down the barrel of the gun at them. Plus I now realised I had maybe forty witnesses to prove I didn't do it. Plus I was on cameras everywhere in Ingleby Barwick. In the end I told the police, to just let me stop them there and to not insult my intelligence because I was miles ahead of them. I told them "if you had any witnesses you'd have me in a line-up straight away." By then I knew that the real suspects where possibly 5ft 7 with ginger hair and black hair with medium build. Well I'm 6ft 3 and 22st stone. Why would I go do a shooting with a dog in a car? If you have witnesses then surely they'll have seen my wife, Ryan and my dog Charlie. They were all completely wasting my time but they'd have to try harder than this shit if they wanted to get Brian Cockerill.

One time the police got me in for an alleged kidnapping charge and they were dancing on the tables thinking we've finally got that fucking Cockerill. All that ended because the guy who was kidnapped went into the police station and said, "It wasn't Brian Cockerill who kidnapped me I only said it because I was off my head on drugs." Cleveland police have tried so many times to get me but they've never been able too.

I was on bail for that murder in Thornaby for seven months and at the end of it I didn't even get an apology. I must say the nice copper Shane said sorry. At one point the coppers were trying to blame my son Jordan but he was at his mates.

Cleveland police were totally unprofessional and it's not the first time I tell you. Going back to a time when Cleveland police had been in my home all day ripping it to pieces convinced I was behind more murders than The Boston Strangler they even had the audacity to keep my gas and electric cards out of sheer spite. They even stole Amanda's cigarettes as they said, "it's part of the investigation" but I think they just made that bit up. When the investigation was all over we never ever got them gas & electric cards, fags, several tracksuits and trainers back so I just told them they could keep the fucking lot.

To be honest I've lost count of how many times they'd pulled strokes like that down to pure vindictiveness. Maybe it comes with the territory of once living in the criminal world but it's also part of the downside to my journey in being the new me and trying to educate the youth of today.

"There's no doubt about it Brian Cockerill is a real fighting man, just like our breed, the travellers. As much as he's a fighting man he's a pure gentleman in equal measures if that makes sense. Brian is a natural born fighting man but that doesn't ever mean he's ever been any kind of bully! The man loved to fight but has never bullied anyone in his life."

Dicky Dido
Stokesley Traveller

CHAPTER 11

FRIENDS AND FALLOUTS

Where do I start with my old friend Terry Dicko apart from saying I'd like to strangle the little bastard for what he wrote about me in his first book 'Laughter, Madness and Mayhem.' No, on a serious note me and Terry were once over extremely close. Today in 2020 we've kissed and made up now and Terry has apologised for what he said about me and I've accepted his apology. Terry had his rant about me when he was angry but for the best part of a quarter of a century we worked well together.

I first met little Terry through Lee Duffy in The Havana. I didn't really get close to Terry until around 1995 when he used to run an illegal unlicensed nightclub named The Steam packet which was located over the border (the St Hilda's area of Middlesbrough) which was an extremely rough place to hang out.

People used to brand the people from the St Hilda's area as "border rats".

As I got more and more familiar with Terry I started going over the border to have a drink with him in his club over there or just a few clubs over there in general. I would say myself and Terry had an instant bond because he was a really likeable funny man. When you're in his company he's a laugh a minute and he's always up to doing crazy things.

Although he's not a fighter as a Viv Graham or a Lee Duffy he is a dangerous little cunt with a weapon and wouldn't think twice about doing something to you if he had something sharp within arm's reach. If you had trouble with Terry Dicko that would only be the beginning of it because it would be your car then your house with it at 4am in the morning. When Terry opened The Steam packet in 1995 it ran until 2003 so he provided the entertainment in Middlesbrough for over eight years when the blues parties shut.

Around the time when Terry had Club Le Packet I was always in there seeing him and that was the time I was fucking massive. In fact I would meet Amanda in Terrys place and we stayed together for over seventeen years. I started seeing Amanda properly when I was on home leave from prison. At the time I was barred out of the whole of Middlesbrough but I was safe in Terry's place because no cops would have had the balls to even enter the place so that's how I started seeing Amanda, it was all down to Terry Dicko.

The very first night I met Amanda in The Steampacket I had a fight with a Middlesbrough boxer called Metty. He was just being too boisterous chewing me not to mention he started on Ray Downing. With me being on home leave from the nick I didn't really want to get into any bother with Metty, even when he was saying that his mate, another boxer from Middlesbrough named Frankie would fill me in. I just told him that he was talking shit and just to piss off away from me but he kept going on and on so I ended up fighting with him . At the time I will have only been around 20st but I was ripped to the bone and super fit with it. Can I just say that when I had a scrap with Metty it was him that threw the first punch but I ended up getting the better of him. When I finished with Metty I turned to his big mate Frankie and shouted, "FUCKING COME ON YOU NOW

BIG MAN" but he didn't want to know. Metty reported me so I ended up getting arrested for it.

Not long after the fight with Metty I went into a fireplace shop over Thornaby and he was in there, it looked like he was hiding from me the whole time I was in the shop but I'd heard he'd been telling everyone he was going to fight me as soon as he clapped eyes on me. I know Metty was telling a legendary old Middlesbrough boxing coach that he was training hard to get his revenge over me even though that boxing coach told him it wasn't a good idea because I'd not long since destroyed former Hartlepool British heavyweight boxer Dave Garside.

I wouldn't bump into Metty again for maybe a couple of months and in that time I'd put another three stone on.

Metty, so I'd been told, had been training for me and I'd heard all the threats so when I saw him in The Steampacket I was like, "NOW THEN GOBSHITE THIS IS GOING TO BE BRILLIANT THIS", so I told him to step outside. There must have been around over one hundred people there such as Terry Dicko, Dave Woodier and Ray Downing when all of a sudden he said, "Bri I'm sorry."

Dave Woodier was working on the door and because of the respect I had for him since he stepped in when I lost to Dave Garside the first time, I left it and I shook Metty's hand but I wish I hadn't now because when I left I heard Metty started on Ray Downing. In fact somebody rang me and said Brian you've got to get back here because Metty's now bullying Ray so I had to drive back and say to him, "YOU TOUCH HIM AND I'LL BREAK YA FUCKING JAW."

Another fight I had in The Steampacket was with another big guy by the name of John T who was 6ft 4 from Thornaby. I was stood at the bar drinking Bacardi and coke with Terry Dicko when John came in and told me to get outside. The reason being the week before, I'd been fighting with two men and I ended up putting both of them to sleep but I actually punched John by accident and I apologised profusely, to which John told me he wasn't accepting my apology so I said alright then we'll have a go and I didn't half fucking muller him and bit right through his nose. Afterwards I heard he said I'd glassed him but I just totally annihilated him and Terry Dicko watched this. Afterwards he said, "fucking hell Brian you've destroyed him."

It must have been from around 1997 that me and Terry Dicko started doing the debts. Terry was incredibly brilliant at finding these jobs because I rarely drank and he spent all his time in the pub all day. A lot of the time if ever I walked in The Steampacket all the proper fighting men of Teesside like your Frankie's and Ste Davies would walk out with their excuses. One lad who would always stay was Docko (God rest his soul) he was a nice lad. The club could hold maybe two-hundred people but when I walked in it would be down to twenty but it wasn't for the same reasons as with Lee Duffy. It was just the reputation I had. To be quite honest the place was full of wrong uns so nine out of ten times there were a lot of drug dealers in there that I'd already taxed at some stage.

The Steampacket was a place where all the rats came to gather. One time when I walked into the packet I shouted, "RIGHT THE RAT CATCHERS BACK AND I'M ROUNDING UP ALL YOU BORDER RATS." It was me just pissing about but all the rats would be scurrying to safety. One thing about Terry Dicko was he's always been hyperactive and has this habit of clicking his hands and putting his legs over people's heads. He'd often try to do it to me and I'd have to say to him, "Terry for fucks sake you're going to kick me on the chin if you don't watch what you're doing." When he was full of ecstasy he'd be even worse. I used to nickname him Terry Klunk from The Wacky Races because of all of his funny little tics.

That time me and Terry fell out I admit I touched him for a few quid and he did the same to me but my excuse for my behaviour was that's what happens when you're on crack cocaine. I could have gone around his house and annihilated him but I would never hurt Terry and if I did what would I achieve? He's my friend. Sometimes he would be funny though as he'd ring me and he'd be like Klunk from The Wacky Races, "YIP YIP YIP ALRIGHT BIG FELLA YIP YIP YIP" and then he'd start to tell me about this ten grand job but I'd be like, "Terry the guy's car is worth £200, he's got holes in his trainers and he doesn't even have any curtains up" so I'd drive away. Sometimes me and Terry went to jobs but at the job a woman would answer the door with maybe five kids, so we'd both say we'd got the wrong house as we couldn't go through with it. We were very much the same in that aspect.

Another job me and Terry went to was near the Junction pub on Union Street but we never got the full story until we arrived. It turns out when we got to the location a sweet old dear opened the door and her son had done away with over six grand of someone's money, or so we thought. What really happened was he'd been arrested with six grands worth of speed and this scumbag dealer who'd called me and Terry in thought we were going to use the strongarm on this family but Brian Cockerill didn't work like that. In my book if you got caught with gear and you kept your mouth shut and took your jail then the debt should be written off and that's what happened. I told that old lady she wouldn't be seeing myself or Terry again and off we went. I told the old dear that if anyone came to her house looking for money then she was to give me a call (I gave her my business card) and to phone me at any time of the day or night.

Another job me and Terry turned up at was in Coulby Newham and it had two big National Frontiers with two Rottweilers but I soon put them in their places. I even shouted at the dogs to sit which they did because I'm also dead good with animals. That job was because these two chancers tried to rip off some elderly gentleman for £400 by selling him some old banger of a car which was an outright fucking liberty.

When I used to arrive at a job I'd be hard but fair and I'd listen to both sides of it. I think the key word to defuse those situations is empathy. Many times I'd be called to defuse certain situations and I'd say to both, you stop doing that, then I'd go back and say to the other, you stop doing this, then whoever does anything after that will have me to answer to. When I came back ok job finished! Both would have probably paid me £200 each and I'd tell them that if I had to come back they would owe me £500.

Certain debt collections or problem solving would be extremely lucrative like the cigarette job because I made £18,000 off that alone. One of Terry Dicko's favourite quotes when we turned up would be 'KNOCK KNOCK' and when they answered he'd say, "we are the naughty people." Every day working with Terry was jovial like he'd be pulling my trousers down and he'd just never be serious for more than two minutes. Another man me and Terry had a lot to do with was Buster (come in car 43) I love Buster to bits but he's not the most switched on person. One day Buster asked me my opinion on something he said, "Brian you're so knowledgeable so what happens if" and he started reeling off about a dozen possibilities that he had and what did I think would happen? In the end I told Buster I didn't know but now I needed two paracetamol because my fucking heads done in (laughs).

Another time Buster was telling me a story which was going on and on and on and I just lost all interest so I said to him that he'd need to hurry up and when he said why? I told him I'd only got three months tax and test on the car. John "Buster" Atkinson I suppose has been a sort of driver for the Middlesbrough underworld as he's been around myself, Lee Duffy, Terry Dicko and Tommy Harrison for the last forty plus years. If you wanted me to sum Buster up he's like Arthur Daley in Minder. Buster would like to think of himself as an old gangster from the 1940's with a Crombie and trilby hat. There's been times that I've been in the middle of nowhere and good old Buster has turned up and he's just such a lovely man.

Going back to Terry Dicko and what he said about me in his first book I think he was going through a bad time with Cleveland police and Tommy Harrison and I got both barrels. They say you take it out on the ones you love but I never meant to hurt him if I did I didn't mean any harm to him. Even though I felt like strangling the little bastard because what he said about me broke my heart. Listen I could rip him to bits now but it's not how I work and I'm a bigger person than that. Not forgetting you ya fucker Jamie Boyle for publishing it!

"When I first met Brian Cockerill I didn't know what to expect as I'd heard so many stories about him. I must say as soon as I was in his company I liked him straight away and his level of intellect really surprised me I'm not going to lie. He's nothing like how he comes across on The Taxman documentary. These days it's great to see the big man has changed his ways and is now helping others."

James English
Podcaster/former model/former professional footballer

CHAPTER 12

THE BEGINNING OF THE END

I suppose the writing was on the wall for me and Amanda for maybe the last five years and in March 2013 she finally had the courage to get up and leave me. Amanda leaving me probably saved both our lives, although I didn't see it like that at the time. One day me and her had been smoking our brains out on the pipe and we'd spent all the mortgage money yet again.

As I've told you all earlier in the book I thought she was worse than me and vice-versa. Today in 2020 I don't want to look back and blame her for any of it because a lot of it was my own doings but at times Amanda stole money.

How she actually left me is a very comical story, what she did was she spiked me by putting sleeping tablets in my drink so she could knock me out, get her stuff and fuck off which is exactly what she did and I've never seen her or my adopted son Jordan since, I brought that kid up from the age of four years of age.

Before Amanda left she stole things out of the house and even money out of rooms, not to mention £650 which she cleared out of my bank account. If you're reading this Amanda I don't blame you and I can understand why you did it but one of the things you tell people about me is I'm a "no-good crack-head." Well the day you left me I know you went to a girls we both know and you bought an 8th of crack cocaine so that wasn't through any involvement with me was it? Apparently you were being pulled down by me and my sinking ship but even when you'd left me you yourself were going to buy the stuff!!! Even a week later she was ringing my friends Phil and Gemma telling them she was off her head and could they pick her up! She apparently asked both for £200 because she was at her sisters down South and she wanted to come home but Phil told her that they wouldn't lend her the money but they'd buy her a train ticket! In the end she didn't take up Phil's offer because it was all bullshit. She just wanted the £200 for more gear. I think even one of them even told Amanda, "I thought it was Brian keeping you on the crack?" I'm not sure how true this is but I've been told she's still into the gear but I wouldn't like to say if that's true or not. I've never seen or even spoken to Amanda or Jordan since March 2013. Jordan took her side because he was her son and only my adopted son and I don't blame the kid.

When I first got in touch with the author of this book Jamie Boyle I told him I was going to be 110% honest for this book and I don't think he believed me.

What I'd like to put in print is I made Amanda's life hell because of the psychosis to the mind which smoking the devil's dandruff brings. One day I brought in over £70,000 in cash and Amanda was in bed but I walked in our room and threw it up in the air like you see in the movies, like I was The Million-Dollar Man. I didn't or wouldn't acknowledge the truth at the time but we were two drug ravaged addicts but with that kind of money we were millionaires. God forgive me for saying this but it's the truth so I will. Me and Amanda sat there for three months and smoked over £70,000 worth of crack cocaine. It's funny how she didn't wanna go then did she? When I was making thousands of pounds from things like my security company and other bits of skulduggery she didn't want to go then! There's an old saying, 'when money goes out of the window love goes with it' and that's what happened with her. When all my money dried up she pissed off sharpish but at the same time I hold my hands up, I wasn't an easy person to live with. I would be constantly shouting at her.

Going back to when I did that 110 days on remand in Holme House in 2011, when I went into Holme House there was over £6,000 in the house, when I got out there wasn't a penny left. Her and Jordan had blown the lot on god knows what! I'm not making excuses up because of how my relationship fell to bits and that's why I'm putting it all in this book. These days I've heard my boy Jordan's favourite thing is to slag me off in public saying I'm just a good for nothing crackhead but that's a bit rich coming from someone who is apparently into everything himself isn't it?! I never ever hit Jordan but he faced me up a few times and I just put him to the floor.

With regards to me and his mother, there shamefully was domestic violence from both of us. I never punched her but I did slap her a handful of times and for that I'm ashamed of myself. For the last seven years I've had no contact with my boy Jordan but it's his choice isn't it. I looked after that boy more than any other kid on the planet, I even got him a job once and he was on £1,250 a week but he fucked it all up. When he was sixteen I got him another job on £400 but he fucked that up also due to his pastimes. The last I heard he's working in Asda now but when he was living with me he was on over £5,000 a month. Even though he was on stupid money all he used to give me and his mam was £20 a week.

If you talk to Amanda and Jordan these days I imagine I'm painted as the fucking devil but we had a lot of good times even if they won't admit it. For the last five years since 2008 we slept in different rooms because she snored really bad so I'd be in the other room with the dog. Towards the end there was no spark with us and we never slept together for over two years as we were more like brother and sister. Most of the time I wouldn't leave the house because I was only too aware of how I looked.

In Terry Dicko's book he says that Amanda would turn up at drug dealers at stupid o'clock but that wasn't exactly true. She did do them things but it was only on my command. When Amanda went on these errands people knew Amanda was Brian Cockerill's Mrs and if anyone even looked at her funny I'd have been over in minutes to wipe them and their armies out. Many times I'd have the gear dropped off by taxi drivers or my old pal Elvis Tomo would sort it. Even back then at that time my confidence was gone and I was a shadow of my former self, I could have still beat anyone. I was a crack ravaged skeleton but I could still fight for fun and I never lost my freakish strength. Amanda used to say when I fought my eyes would go black and she never liked looking at me like that. I'm not talking about fighting with her I'm on about the dozens of street fights she saw me involved with.

Amanda was with me one night when we were in a house with six other men but I battered every one of them senseless. I'm not talking about average Joes I'm talking about six big men. One of the men I left hooked and he was twitching on the floor and I thought I'd killed him or he was swallowing his tongue but what was really happening was he was choking on the blocks of crack he'd hid in his mouth just before I arrived. Needless to say I took them out of his mouth and kept them for his own safety of course.

Going back to my seventeen-and-a-half-year relationship with Amanda, as far as I know she was loyal and never cheated on me and also so was I. I took her to Greece and that's where I proposed to her with a £1,000 engagement ring. It was worth a hell of a lot more as I got a deal from Alan Goodchild's jewellers in Middlesbrough and we had such a fantastic time.

During them dark times of 2013 I must say I need to give a special mention to my sister Catherine and say a huge thank you. When I used to bullshit her ringing her asking for money saying it was for my mortgage she never questioned me. 99.99% it was usually a lie and it would be for drugs. I owe my sister Catherine everything and much more than money let me tell you. At times my sister Catherine has rang me frequently asking if I'm ok and I've said, "of course I am you dozy cow." Only when she's calmed down she's told me it was all over Facebook that Brian Cockerill had just received 10-20 years for armed robbery! Another time our Catherine has rang screaming that I let her know I'm ok because it's all over the internet that big Bri's choked to death on a chicken bone. I told her there's nothing wrong with me and that I'm at home with Bobby and Scrappy-Doo watching telly. Another story that somebody heard was that I died of a heart-attack on a beach in Spain. At one point even my mates Cleveland police turned up and knocked at the door, my ex Amanda can verify this, anyway the police needed to visually see me ASAP because they'd heard I'd been murdered. I hadn't been murdered but was I fuck letting them see me in the state I was in at the present as I'd just finished piping my brains out. The police told Amanda that what they'd heard was a really naughty Liverpool firm had had me done in as there was a contract put on my head. In the end I had to walk down in my dressing gown looking like Beetlejuice for seconds just to prove I wasn't at the bottom of the Mersey.

The week before Amanda left me I taxed £4,000 so I give Amanda £2,000 and told her to pay the mortgage which she never. What she actually did was paid only £20 but added a couple of 0's on the end of it. What she was really doing was saving up to leave me which she did only one week later. I won't lie, Amanda was my complete rock and the love of my life for the whole time we were together. Please don't think I'm being big headed when I say this because I'm not trying to say I'm Mr handsome, I'm just not that confidant with the opposite sex but I had some really top models coming on to me because of who I was, Brian Cockerill the celebrity of Teesside. There was one stunning girl from Darlington who tried it on with me but I told her I don't mess about. Amanda was my everything and I was loyal to a fault. I've only slept with two woman in over twenty-three years. Today in 2020 I'm only 55 so if god doesn't drop a piano on my head or strike me down with lightening then I'd like to think I'm only two-thirds through my life so I'm glad that the big fella sent me my Emma to spend the rest of my days with.

The one thing I do know is I've well and truly cleaned my act up as far as the narcotics side of things go and I never want to go back to them dark days ever again because it almost killed me.

If you're reading this Amanda then I wish you all the best and I'm sorry for all the fights we had. I hope you can remember it wasn't all bad. Sometimes in life love hits the rocks (not them kinda rocks). Regarding my son Jordan he did hear a lot of shouting and bawling between his mam and me and we were both on drugs so I suppose nobody wants their Mam to live that life do they?! What I'd like to go on record to say is the reason I used to shout at his Mam was that I had my suspicions that she was thieving off me and in the end my thoughts regarding that were confirmed to be true so there you go. I had my suspicions that Jordan himself was taking £20 a day off me for years. In fact one day I found over a grand that he'd hidden. One day he came in with about £40 worth of Pokeman cards and when I quizzed him about it he said they were his mates. The sad thing is that boy never needed to take anything from me, I used to give him £20 a day to go to school! Another thing was he had the best of everything from me clothes wise and he'd also be taking my phones and then going out getting mouthy with people so I'd have to fight his battles. One incident I remember was that Jordan told me that some older lad had hit him for nothing so obviously I went around to the premises for a civil conversation and before the occupants could even open the door there were twenty-five police officers about. If the average Joe Public went to that door they wouldn't have even bothered turning up.

Another incident regarding how over the top the police were with me was when I went to a naughty property where they had been selling crack to kids. Now I know what you're thinking here, that I'm a fine one to talk, well the truth is yes I've taken crack but I've never sold it. In fact I've been offered tens of thousands of pounds to sell it but I've always told them to fuck off! If you trade in smack or crack you're working for the devil. If you're in that game you're responsible for old people being robbed and young kids having their bikes taken off them the lot. It's not for me, yes it's been alleged I was involved in the trafficking of ecstasy, speed and a bit of blow but that's as far as I went.

Anyway, going back to this house which three of us went to. When we got there there was about ten blokes and a lot of them were gypsies and real fighting men. In fact one of them was named, "trout-head" who set his lip up so I grabbed him and I was going to kidnap him and put him in the boot of the car. When I was chatting to this gang they told me this location which had £40,000 of cash there and two kilos of coke so we were all planning on going with my new hostage/best mate. Well you wouldn't believe my luck as just before we were ready to head off and go collecting, the boys in blue with their flashing lights and loud wailing sirens turned up screaming asking what's going on? Looking back one of the neighbours must have reported some funny goings on. Anyway when the police turned up one of the officers shouted, "ITS BRIAN COCKERILL" then instantly radioed in for the cavalry and two dozen of the biggest officers turned up within two-three minutes. It was all a long time ago now but I do remember screaming at the police that these bastards are selling crack cocaine to kids and for vermin like these you've sent half the shift out against Brian Cockerill!!!

Another time I was arrested for taking a kilo of coke from some Nigerian in Coulby Newham. Here's a true fact for you regarding myself, I was the first person in British history to be arrested by the usual armed response for taking drugs off vermin drug dealers which is ludicrous. That Nigerian was bringing the drugs in the country and I'm just relieving him of them so who's the worst??? That even almost went to court until the Judge kicked it out. For that I was put in a police line-up and at the time I was almost 24st and the people in the line-ups were bald and 5ft 4 so it was obvious they just wanted me to go down but thank god that Judge saw sense and it didn't get that far is all I can say.

I've also had seven powder residue tests for murders here, there and everywhere but all have been clear. One police officer actually said to me, "Brian you're either the unluckiest man in the world to have been arrested for all these things or you really know your stuff and cover your tracks professionally."

I represented myself on three occasions in 1994 and got NOT GUILTY on every single occasion in Teesside Magistrates.

Another time I was pulled in for three separate shootings in The Blue Monkey rave club in Stockton and that was nothing to do with me either.

After Amanda left me though in 2013 I went through a period of not leaving my home for over six months because I knew I looked that bad. Then when I started going back out I'd go to do the shopping at like Tesco at 4am. Not to mention my confidence was shattered as well as my paranoia was through the roof. Maybe I deserved it but I was going through my own living hell and was totally on my own.

"Listen I've now personally chosen this new path, but don't be fooled, there's life in this old dog and I'm not ready to be put to sleep just yet."

Brian Cockerill

CHAPTER 13

I'M GOING TO MAKE YOU AN OFFER YOU CAN'T REFUSE

Over my criminal career I've been approached by several police forces many times to come on the side of law and order. The words they always use is, "we can help you if you help us", they always seem to be the magic words.

The time I was in custody for allegedly robbing hardened drug dealers of their ill-gotten gains I was put in a line-up but I wasn't picked out. After I wasn't picked out I started getting annoyed telling them I wanted to be let out this very second as they had stolen enough of my time. I was told to calm down but I said, "fuck being calm I'm innocent so let me the fuck out" but before I was let out I was approached sideways if you like. In fact one of the inspectors told Amanda's uncles one day in the fishing shop he owned over Thornaby, he said "no wonder Brian Cockerill hates the police as some of them used to torture that poor man." Nobody else in the world used to be hounded like I was by the police and even my old solicitor Craig Bier (God rest him) used to say the same.

Sometimes several officers used to carry law books on them and study them thoroughly just in case to see if they could find something to hold me on.

I would say that because I'd beaten the police many many times on charges then that's when it started to become a personal vendetta against me. After years of them trying to put me away and them failing then that's when I started being pulled in with the old, "you don't fancy working for us do ya?" Like they were chat-up lines.

I'll tell you something now, you wouldn't believe just how many leading figures of the criminal underworld are actually on the payroll with Cleveland police let me tell you first-hand. One day when I was trying to be turned one of the elder more well-known top police figures heard what was going on and before this officer could finish trying to get me to sell my soul he shouted, "OOR YOU'RE NOT TRYING TO TURN COCKERILL ARE YOU BECAUSE YOU'VE GOT NO FUCKING CHANCE TRYING TO TURN HIM", and he was right.

Since Lee Duffy turned me to the dark side and I became some sort of criminal I was always a one side of the fence type of guy. Even when the police have begged me telling me, "Brian nobody will ever find out," I've told them "I'm not a rat." I used to say to them that they'd know and I'd fucking know. Then because I wouldn't conform he said, "well you know them driving offences I'm going to make sure you go to jail but if you do as I say I'll make sure I can get that quashed for you." I just told them I'd rather get twenty years then when I got out I could walk down the street with my head held high. I told them you might have all these other scumbags on board but I'm like James Cagney in those old films and I have morals.

Wherever I've been or whoever I've worked with like the people from Redcar, Stockton, Newcastle, Leeds and Manchester then I've always been ok. It's only when I worked with lads from Middlesbrough that the police were on to me and followed me everywhere. I had bugs in my house and car it was ridiculous. I'll say one thing about my old friend Lee Duffy though and that was that he had good morals and he was a cardboard cut out of me. I know for a fact that never in his life did Lee Duffy ever make a statement to the law. Davey Allo got off with Lee's murder and that's how Lee Duffy would have wanted it. Even his mother Brenda told the press that's exactly what he would have wanted and that's 100% bang on accurate in how I knew Lee Duffy.

Even when the police quizzed The Duffer over who shot him he told them all to fuck off! That was the man. If you want the truth then the handful of times I've been approached by the old bill its fabulously offended me. In fact its fucking disgusted me truth be known but I want you to know it does happen. I could put some very well-known peoples name in here from Teesside that I know who've done it because they've got no morals. You know, I can go to bed on a night and sleep peacefully knowing I've never made a statement to the police and put anyone in prison. There's not one policeman that could come forward and prove anything other than what I'm telling you for this book. Don't get me wrong I used to hate the police and I'm talking about the corrupt kind who took bribes from the people like Brian Charrington etc.

I've met a hell of a lot of corrupt bent police and you know the reason why? It's because we're in Middlesbrough which is the capital of bent police forces in Britain. Yes I've been approached by naughty police officers but I think a lot of them were put off with asking me because they wouldn't deal with me and I'd have ruined them even if I'd have said yes which I wouldn't have in the first place. The average PC will pull you out of a burning car or if you fall in a river he'll save your life if you're drowning and I've learnt first-hand not all of them are bad. There's good baddies and bad goodies like myself.

One police officer who lives near to me knocked on my door and asked, "Bri you couldn't help us could you?" Straight away I told him I couldn't make a statement but he went on, "listen this old lady has been robbed of everything out of her bungalow etc etc." To cut a long story short seven hours later I got every single thing back for her and that was down to just pure word on the street. It was down to the criminal grapevine and I didn't take, nor did I want a penny for shit like that. One time like that the same thing happened to Amanda's mam and dad and I got the whole lot and even the car back. Since I've been living in Ingleby Barwick nobody dare burgle on my street.

When I went to prison all hell broke loose because Ingleby Barwick is the biggest housing estate in the whole of Europe with 21,000 people living there. When I was on the out the crime rate was 14% whereas when I went inside the local beat bobby on his bike told Amanda that the rates where now up to 77% for crime. The officer was even asking Amanda when I was getting back out and was even worried he was going to lose his job.

"When I've been in the schools with Brian when he's been doing his talks the kids are glued to him. They'll roll their eyes at Mrs Smith and put their thumbs in their ears when Mr West tries to speak with them but when Brian talks these kids are glued to his every word and that's a thing which normally you would think is so so wrong. For instance, I wouldn't want my son looking up to Brian Cockerill or glamorising him, but the reality is Brian Cockerill has had a life where he's made thousands of mistakes for them to learn from. Brian, in truth, completely fucked up all his prospects and now he's here trying finally to do good and to talk some sense into the youth of Teesside."

Jamie Boyle

CHAPTER 14

BECOMING A SOMEBODY

There's no point in me doing chapters and chapters of myself and weight training, diets and discipline in this book because I'm going to be doing a full book purely on that 100% with Jamie Boyle soon.

I wasn't just green in the drugs world I was green in the gyms across Teesside when I first started. Although I'm an expert in my field it wasn't always the case and once upon a time I was pissing in the wind.

I was doing things in gyms and breaking world records such as when I was in Moore's gym in Stockton and Addish, Ali and Mark Johnson and Kevin Kilty were there. I did seven reps of 2000lbs which is the weight of a car, Mark and Paul Epstein the owners of the gym were there once and I shouted, "HELP" and everyone in the gym ran over panicking only for me to say, "I'm only fucking joking."

When I was in Holme House in 2011 I broke the 1,500-leg press and that was me being an old man. In Fact the ex-drug dealer Bud Armstrong, Dean Wilson, Mark Owens, Richy Bowser and Mark Davison were there that day. Everyone in the gym that day stopped to watch me in amazement but I know half of them were thinking, he's doing too much here he's going to flop.

I was with Steel City owner Micky Lawrence only the other day and he even reminded me of the time I busted a machine by leg pressing over 2000lbs when I was about 26.

Back in those days nobody was doing that and I broke a world record there and then.

Chrissy Mulcaster used to spot me with 630lbs and I'd even get a touch on 700lbs I couldn't do it because the bar was bending. In those days I could squat 800lbs and even Dave Taylor (one half of the famous Boro comedy duo Bob & Dave) used to wonder how the fuck could I lift that weight?!

What I will say is people know that Brian Cockerill has had his addictions in life but believe me when I say this, training has always been my biggest addiction.

Today in 2020 I still train twice a day in my own gym at home on my own regimes. Years ago Brian Cockerill was all about monstrous weights whereas today I do much lighter weights but more reps. See when your young your muscles and joints can take it but now I'm getting on if I was to lift what I did back in my heyday I'd only gain injuries daily. If you lift big you need more Carbohydrates and protein because you need the carbs in your body. I meet a lot of people today who don't really have a clue in regards to what it takes to be an elite strong man like I was. Rest is maybe the biggest thing and these young kids who I talk too often in gyms don't give themselves time to recover. Back in 1986 I competed for the Mr England (even though I'm Scottish I know) and I came 5th.

Back in those days training was everything to me it was my whole life! In reality, and truth be told, when I went for the Mr England title I didn't have a clue what I was doing with my diet. I would diet for maybe ten days when everyone in it was dieting for ten weeks. I still looked good but that's the reason why I failed. Those were the shows were you caked yourself in all the fake tan and you look like an umpa-lumpa so the judges can see your definition etc… I wouldn't only be doing those shows I was into all sorts like pulling trucks for charity. That truck weighed six and a half ton and I pulled it by myself for three miles when everyone else was taking turns. I was only twenty-one so pulling that truck for the three miles just shows how fit I was. I was at my peak in training around the time Lee Duffy walked up and punched me in the face for nothing. At that exact time I was around 23st 10lbs and I looked awesome which was really the reason that Lee did it in the first place to make a statement when he thought he was going to knock me out. At that time Duffy was only around 15st 7lbs and the biggest he ever got was 17st 9lbs when Craig Howard got him on the gear when he was training to have a fight with me.

The facts are that there must have been an easy 8st difference between me and him that day and that was the reason I could easily manhandle him with ease after he smacked me. Think of a flyweight taking on a heavyweight it's the exact same weight difference. Lee, even when he was 15st, could put men out cold just like Deontay Wilder is now so Duffy could hit no matter what weight he was really. Believe me he punched like a motherfucker!

Many years ago I was only about powerlifting whereas today in 2020 and being 55 years old I'll maybe use 10kg dumbbells which I'll use one hundred times. The training even still today gives me natural endorphins which keeps my mind healthy, not to mention keeps my body fat down. These days I get up on a morning and have my breakfast which is normally a bowl of cornflakes with no sugar and a cup of coffee, then one hour later I'll have 100 grams of porridge with 50 grams of a protein shake. Another hour later I'll have two eggs with one slice of granary bred and low-fat butter. An hour later I'll have another protein shake and it goes on like that every two hours. Dinner is normally steak, pork chops or chicken with salad, rice or potatoes and three or four different types of veg. Also at the same time I take vitamin B, D and multi-vitamins with cod liver oil.

After I train then I need to put more stuff into my body. When you put your body through this you lose what is called glycogen which is your energy source in your liver. If you don't put the proper stuff back into your body it can take 36 hours to regain it and that's why the next day you're in the gym and you might have felt great the day before but now you're fucked. That's the reason why, so I make sure I always do things properly even though my competing days are long gone. Your body is like a mobile phone and if you don't charge it properly it's not going to work so that's why it's so important to look after yourself properly.

Eating a banana holds over 200 grams of potassium and that helps to lower your blood pressure because it's full of sodium. When you eat banana's that alone puts the glycogen back in your liver. When you've done a heavy session in the gym your body is screaming out for the glycogen to be put back into your body. As bad as I was with the crack, I still trained when I could because out of the two the training was my biggest addiction and maybe that is why I'm still here.

That time I was set upon by a dozen or so heavies in Tommy Harrison's old house up Ormesby Bank the only reason I'm still here now is because I was so big. All that 23st of muscle cushioned the blows to the point I didn't even have one broken bone, although I had holes all over me and 176 stitches and so on.

The people who watched my documentary on Macintyre's could visually see my tics and OCD but training has been like that with me also. Some people are gamblers, alcoholics, swingers, doggers etc well I had the same addiction but with training. From when I watched Arnold Schwarzenegger's Pumping Iron film as a young boy that shaped my life and pointed me into the path I chose in sport. I wanted to be like Arnie and trained day and night to be like him. People reading this must think because I'm now a big fella I must have been a big kid but I was the opposite. For a start I had asthma and it was that bad I nearly died when I was very young. Also I was born with a dislocated hip and I walked with a limp for years so that was another thing I was picked on for.

When I was young we moved about a lot also and I lived in places such as North Ormesby, Redcar and Hartlepool and it didn't get any better in any of those places I went to. My mam was a really bad alcoholic and my dad was very much into gambling so I didn't have the best starts in life so training helped me escape this living hell I was trapped in.

I went to a special school in Hartlepool because I couldn't read and write. Often people would laugh at me saying I was a window licker and they'd tell me to get back to my "spacka school." When I'd tell people I was now in my school football team and I was the captain I'd be ridiculed even more and I was told I was the leader of the spacka's.

If I went home and told some of my family members I'd passed my 50 metres at swimming I'd be laughed at and asked, "what do you want a medal for it?" I really had no encouragement at all for anything positive that I did and my brothers were the same. As kids me and Bobby were told our house was haunted so are you surprised a few of us grew up with issues?!

As a boy I'd watch Jason and the Argonauts and all the old films were you'd see these big strong monsters and looking back I would say that deeply influenced me. I started with the kids films first then that developed to sitting in front of the telly watching bodybuilders and I knew that one day I was going to be like that. Another thing I was glued to as a kid was Minder. I'd watch Terry McCann and think, I wish I could fight like him and not be bullied.

It was in my early teens that I first started going into the weightlifting gyms in Hartlepool and training. Back at that time I didn't have a clue what I was doing and it was all guess work. As a kid my nickname was "puggy" because I had a little tiny nose. My uncles would often grab my nose and say, "Alright wee Puggy?!"

Anyway one of my Mam's brothers owed her some money put he couldn't afford to pay her back so he said to my mam one day, "if I give our puggy these weights is that us evens" and he gave me these made up weights, the rest is history as they say. The weights that started me off were 160lbs in total. My uncle wasn't any kind of expert in training but he started showing me as a 14-year-old boy what to do with these weights. I had half an idea anyway because I used to watch Arnie in Pumping Iron daily.

Back in those days I used to think, the more you do the bigger you get but it's not! You should do a solid twenty minutes then rest until the next day. When I was say 15 I'd train 3-4 times a day I was obsessed with it wanting to be like my hero's and not be bullied anymore and in time that stopped. When I left school I was 6ft 1 and already getting into some fantastic shape. I didn't really put the bulk on until I moved to Redcar when I was 18 years old. When I moved to Redcar I was a big lad but I had no confidence at all and the reason was is I'd been bullied and put down all my life. As a young man I really didn't have any confidence at all because all my life I'd been told I was useless and known as Brian from the 'spacka' school so why would I have any confidence? After a while you start to believe it don't you?!

I would say I didn't come out of my shell until I got my little flat in Redcar and started working on the doors. In my spare time the only thing I did was go to a gym and that's where I met a man named Peter Ayton from Redcar. Peter was only about 5ft 7 but he reminded me of something like out of Arnie's film Pumping Iron he was awesome for his size. Although he was small, his arms were massive and I don't mind admitting I was overawed because at that time I was only 11st 10lbs but that's when I really took my training to the next level. When all the people I knew were out taking drugs and boozing I was in the gym or eating porridge and that's when I began to bulk.

Within two years of my training I'd put three stone on. I know that because when I started working for John Black on Leo's door I was 14st 10lbs. When I first started the doors I worked with a man named Frankie Atherton (sadly passed in 2019) and the club was owned by Peter and Phil Lyons and it was located on Redcar sea front. I got the job on that door and I was fighting all the time with it but still as green as grass. It was Frankie who first started showing me a few pugilistic moves. Up until then I didn't know or have a clue how to fight. I was strong and good at grabbing people and carrying them outside in full nelsons but that's all I could do. If anyone started throwing punches at me all I knew to do was choke them out, I didn't have a clue how to deliver a punch. It was around that time that someone suggested I take up boxing so that's exactly what I did and I went to Lingdale ABC which was ran by an old legendary coach named Ray Hood (also sadly passed in 2019) and he taught me the basics of boxing. Well after maybe 6-7 weeks of boxing I knew how to fight alright and everybody was talking about this young kid on Leo's door. If I'm going to be honest with you I wasn't the world's greatest amateur boxer. I trained at Ray's for one year and only had one amateur bout which I lost on points but what I did take away from that training was the fundamental basics of boxing which I moulded into my street fighting. Now not only could I strangle the life out of people if needs be I could stand and let basic combinations go.

Going back to the amateur boxing and the fight I lost, I was put in the ring with a lad who'd been boxing for over six years with many contests so he was vastly more experienced than me. Looking back I did well to even go the distance but because I was so heavy I had to go in with these guys if I was wanting to compete. I was just that big it was hard to get matched.

Looking at my weight training which is what I was doing at the same time as the boxing I trained at The Chapel Gym which was owned by Anthony Berg who was an ex-army lad. In fact he gave me a job in there so he was paying me £20 a week but I was also training there for free. With me now training for free that's when I really started to excel because I could really go for it.

At that time in my life in Redcar I had lots of little jobs at the same time like being camp patrol on a site nearby and also a car park attendant not to mention working at Redcar

Racecourse. Back in that time every penny I made went on bodybuilding supplements. I also worked in a video shop for £1 per hour as well as window cleaning or pissing about fixing cars. I did anything to help me become a monster like out of Jason and the Argonauts. I didn't even like the taste of alcohol and you all know what I went on to become in life but at that time I wasn't even so much as crossing the road on a red light. In fact I tell a lie I once got done for not having my L plate on a motorbike once when I first got it.

In the gym it was Terry Cooper and Peter Ayton who really took me under their wing and started to show me what I should be doing. These guys were competing as bodybuilders and knew their shit so I was all ears. There's people today in Redcar who remember Brian Cockerill who was built like a lat. My uncle Tam used to tell people how one day I was going to be big but people would often come back and tell him I didn't have the natural genetics. One day I was watching Tom Platz the American professional bodybuilder and I told everyone who I was watching it with that I was going to get legs as big as him and everybody laughed at me. My uncle Tam would tell anyone who'd listen that his little Puggy was going to be the biggest thing ever to come out of Teesside. I don't know why but uncle Tam knew I had that potential.

There was no greater feeling in life for me at that time when I was growing at a ridiculous rate like 13st – 14st – 15st etc etc at an alarming rate. I didn't need sex the training was better than any of that nonsense could ever offer me.

Another man I met at that time in Redcar was George Fawcett who'd competed in loads of bodybuilding competitions and he even started training me. I lived close by to George in the Lakes Estate of Redcar. I used to copy every one of George's moves and he became a role model for me at that time. It was George who first said to me, "Brian I think you can compete yourself soon" and that was music to my ears but I didn't quite believe what he was saying because I still lacked the confidence. Anyway it was George who took over my diet and showed me just how to put my tan on. It was around that time I moved to The Olympia gym on Redcar sea front and that place was just full of the elite men of the area. The place was run by a man named Don Williams and his son was Dave Williams who was classed as the Mike Tyson of Redcar who could fight every fucker. Dave even beat Peter Hoe who could really fight for fun so that showed the level of violence he could dish out. Dave Williams was like a big lion and around 18st himself but only around 5ft 8 in height. Apart from his height everything was huge on Williams i.e. barrel chested, he was built like a fucking tank and he was the king of Redcar. I'll never forget, it was the 7th of March 1987 and it was the same night James "Bonecrusher" Smith fought a Mike Tyson. Craig Howard was always sniffing around Dave Williams because he had a name and that's just what Craig Howard did as I've already told you earlier with me and Lee Duffy. I don't know why Craig Howard was the way he was because he competed for the Mr Universe, in fact if you type in his name on YouTube you can see him on there for yourself he really did look the mutts nuts but saying that he couldn't fight.

It was Craig Howard who introduced me to Dave Williams. Craig introduced me as Brian Cockerill and I was a bodybuilder to look out for and that I was the best fighter in Leo's nightclub. It was then that Dave Williams said to me, "what do you do in Leo's are you a glass collector son?" Well straight away I thought, you cheeky cunt! It was in the stars it was going to come off between me and him from then on which I'll tell you about further on in this book. This was around the time I was really becoming cocksure of myself.

I was strong, I could box but the only problem was this was Dave Williams who was the hardest man in Redcar so doubt crept in my mind. Yes I was bullied but when I was at school I was beating people 20 years old. Although I didn't have any confidence I was the best fighter in all the areas I lived in. I made a promise to myself around 13-14 years old that I wouldn't allow myself to be bullied anymore and I'd stand up for myself which is what I went on to do. The bullying was at an all-time worst between 9 and 11 years old then when I started fighting back I thought, this is better than running away all the time. Every single day of my life I'd plan my route home with military precision. I'd think, if I run across the railway lines today then six lads wont kick the fuck out of me. Many times that pack of hyenas caught me on the beach and I took my medicine and that's why it angers me when people who've never even met me say, "oh that big Bri Cockerill's nothing but a fucking bully!" You know what, nothing could be further from the truth because I know what it's like to get the daily beatings for nothing so regarding that comment I don't fucking think so.

You know, me usually having the shit kicked out of me daily meant that I turned into a terrible liar also. I would go around saying my dad's a millionaire or an army man, or even my mam knows the Queen, those kind of lies, there was logic behind them, it was all to try and save myself. I would often tell anyone who's listen I was a master in 'Hong Kong Phooey' and if needs be I could be deadly with it. Now you probably all remember the dog who dressed in a karate suit that went around and battered people from

1974 in the children's cartoon, I told people it wasn't just a cartoon but my parents took me to learn the ancient art of Hong Kong Phooey so people better be careful around me. The odd couple of occasions some kids believed me and I'd be left alone, most the time I'd be asked to demonstrate for their sheer entertainment then when they realised I was telling lies then that would end up with a kicking Hong Kong Phooey himself would have been proud of and I'd receive a few karate chops to the neck.

I've been everything in life i.e. having to run, being scared, fight for my life and I was the hide and seek champion. Once upon a time I was just little Puggy with no confidence so when I started to stand up for myself I became the best fighter in my school out of about 160 kids. I was known as the best fighter in Hartlepool but I never bullied anyone and there's a difference.

Going back to The Olympia gym I thought I'd made it. I used to have thirty raw eggs a day and I could eat like a pig (some say I haven't changed). Eating eggs is better than any other kinds of protein along with milk. I would say because I went to the Olympia gym and now I was being trained by George that was the reason I did eventually go to the level of competing in the Mr England. It was when I was there that I met this great big huge black guy named Vince Brown who was Mr Universe and he kept staring at me so when he came over and told me that my posing was, "absolutely spot on son and you've got a physique like Arnold Schwarzenegger." Well hearing stuff like that I couldn't believe it, and that was before the time I'd even taken a steroid when everyone else in that Mr England show was on them. When I entered that competition I had a 26inch waist and 44inch chest and I was 20years old. I would never take a steroid until I was 22 and it was Mark Lenny who showed me the ropes. People think that the juice is the be all and end all in training but it's not. You don't stop growing until your 21 when your plates fuse. That's when you don't get any taller. If anyone's reading this and thinking about taking steroids then please listen to me, you shouldn't take any steroids until you've finished growing at 21. You have a growth hormone release but that stops producing at 32. Every year after that it goes down by 1% which is why you start getting wrinkles and you get fat then your testosterone levels drop and you go downhill unless you train like mad. If you train it slows down the process but nobody can stop father time, not even Brian Cockerill. That's why you should train and look after yourself then you're 10-15 years younger than people your own age.

When I did so well in the Mr England all my family were crying with joy and I really was ripped to the bone but I knew then the only way to become even bigger was to get on the roids. Around that time I was travelling around Britain going in other bodybuilding comps such as Mr Skegness and a few others but what I was finding out in these comps was it was all fixed. What I mean is I heard one of the judges saying to one of my fellow competitors that if he bought all his protein now from his company he'll make sure he gets the 1st place so I fucked it off. I thought all these daft little shows like the Mr England's were a load of shit and to fuck it off, not to mention I'm Scottish of course so now I was going to become the world's strongest man, fuck these amateurs I thought! That's why I became like The Incredible Hulk and took every strongman spinach like Popeye on this planet. Steroids or not I leg-pressed over 2000lbs in front of Kevin Kilty and Mark Johnson.

When I was training in The Olympia they were doing this thing which was whoever could lift the most then we'd name that machine after them. Well I had my name on every single machine in that gym. Nobody could come anywhere near to Brian Cockerill and you can ask Mark Langy, George Fawcett, Mark Debrick, Liam Henry or anyone who went to Body Matters gym in Middlesbrough. I have it all on video which I'll be putting on my documentaries so for anyone who thinks that Brian Cockerill is back on the gear talking tall stories you can watch it yourself. I was squatting 500lbs and benching 400lbs when I was twenty years old and that was with no steroids.

One day I went to a gym in Guisborough and there was a powerlifter who was a fully mature man in there who was on the GB team and he was squatting 600lbs, well that day I was in there at twenty and I was doing 500lbs at only twenty years old as I've said, so that showed my potential. That guy at the time was 26st by the way.

If you're reading this and you're thinking, well what's the most you've ever lifted Brian then the answer to that is 803lbs which is 365kg. I did three reps on that. I've front squatted seven plates either end which is around 300kg and I did six reps. I used to be able to do back squat six and a half plates which is around 280kg and I did twenty reps. Funnily enough it was a policeman who spotted me in the gym for that. Now there's an argument that that's nowhere near the Olympic standard but its world class and ask anyone to confirm what I'm saying if they know anything about weightlifting!

When I used to watch the world's strongest man on the telly I'd then get motivated and go into the gym and beat what they'd just done. I'm not making this up and that's how good I was but of course I thought Brian knew best and blew the lot by being a professional criminal. My peak years were when I was 24-28 years old and that's when I could have beaten anyone in the world!

One particular time I went down Sheffield to see strongman Jamie Reeves and when I was there just spectating some of the other strongmen saw me then said to all the other competitors that day saying, "ere lads come and have a look at this fucker here" and then there was like a dozen strongmen stood all around me checking me out. This might sound crackers but that's how I got an invite to compete in the world's strongest man from just all of those guys looking at me. A few asked what I could do and I was using 63kg dumbbells in each arm curling them.

Paul (R.I.P) and Mark Debrick were also two really strapping lads from Boro who could easily bench 300lbs each. Paul once rang me about six months before he died from the rigs having a right whinge because nobody would train with him because everybody on the whole rig wanted to watch my Donal Macintyre documentary.

"I love all these haters I get because when you take the time out of your day to write your negative comments then you're giving me attention. In fact you're only helping me with the sales for my books by giving me any kind of attention so crack on. All you haters out there just keep hating me because I love it."

Brian Cockerill

CHAPTER 15

THAT 'G' WORD

I've always been well known since the late 1980s but in truth anyone who knows me will know I shy away from the limelight. Especially the gangster tag which Brian Cockerill has been attached to for the last 30 years.

When I was filming Faces of the Underworld with Bernard O'Mahoney I had a lot of invites from well-known associates such as Pretty Boy Roy Shaw, Mad Frankie Fraser and Dave Courtney all saying, "when are we going to meet this big bastard?!"

Of course at times I've been extremely close to well-known villains like Stephen and Michael Sayers who are both extremely nice lads. These days they've turned their lives around and good on them. Stephen, like me is happy to talk about his past as long as people learn from it and it's not glamorised. Michael tends to shy away and lives the quiet life but Michael was the crazy one but I mean that in the nicest possible way. Michael is fucking bonkers and he was maybe closer than anyone to Lee Duffy as they were both sentenced to four years on March 23rd, 1987 and went right through their jail terms together to places like Durham and Armley. Michael is mad as a March hare and Jamie Boyle who is writing this book has met a kindred spirit in Michael because he's fucking crackers as well.

What I'd like to say about the Sayers family is they're as genuine as they come. If you were stuck and needed helping out, it didn't matter if you were on the moon they'd come and help you out if they respected you. John, Stephen and Michael I have all the love in the world for as well as their wider family such as Eddie Lennie and Tony Sayers Snr. People outside of the criminal fraternity may think people like myself, the Sayers, Lee Duffy and even the likes of Roy Shaw and Lenny McLean are all pure scum but the bottom line is some of that might be true but none of them named above liked to see kids or animals getting hurt. If you look at people like myself, Lenny McLean, Roy Shaw and Lee Duffy we were all bullied and I'm sure I could name more names that were the same.

Another thing I've noticed in Britain over the last few years is that all the top fighters such as Lenny McLean, Ernie Bewick and Viv Graham all have had unique and strange names, it's never been like Tommy Smith etc…

Ernie Bewick can I just say is one really fantastic man who's never been beat by anyone. He's an absolute legend in Sunderland were he's from and just in the whole of the North in general. I'd never ever fight with Ernie because I love him like a brother but in another book Steve Richards said that I went up to Sunderland to fight Ernie. Can I just say for the record that I never said anything of the sort! I said I fought a guy the size and build of Ernie but Steve Richards added little bits of crap for sales to flourish.

One-time Mad Frankie Fraser was in Sunderland at a book signing and he was always asking the doorman about me and asking if they had a number for me. He did it on another two visits to the North East but sadly I never got to meet him and that's one thing I do regret because he certainly had some life. Dominic Noonan was another who was always asking Donal Macintyre when he was going to meet me. The Noonan family with his other brothers Damian and Dessie ran a lot of Manchester. Dominic did a feature programme like me with Donal Macintyre but back in 2005 he was arrested in Darlington with a gun and 5 bullets with a couple of young boys. He was coming down to shoot a well-known Darlo man I knew very well.

These days Dominic is doing double figures for sex offences and his name is worse than shit.

I was in jail with Paul Massey's brother also. It wasn't just the criminals in society that were drawn to me. My mate Pecca got a phone call once from a former Sunderland and England striker who had lost this 100K watch in some deal and he was going to give me half the money but for legal reasons I didn't get involved. There was another England international wanting to meet me abut I never went to see him. He sent several messages and in the end I sent him some signed posters of me but I regret that now as well.

That's what I was like all the time down to drugs and just wasting some top opportunities and foots in the door which could have led onto bigger things.

People have often asked me why these famous millionaires want to meet Brian Cockerill from the council estates! My friends have told me it's because of what I have done in life was unique and unusual which I can see their points. My mates when answering that question to people have said, "there's Batman, Spiderman, Superman and The Taxman runs along with them."

There's loads who've tried to follow me and lost their lives. When I was doing it it was fucking dangerous and there had to be a load of money in it for it to be worth the risk. Back in my heyday you really had to be able to fight because there weren't guns like there is now and there wasn't as much knife crime.

When me and Lee Duffy were about if you weren't good with your fists you couldn't tax a gram off anybody. Can you imagine what kind of bottle it takes to go to some violent drug dealers door on your own. I wasn't stupid I knew that my enemies were laying in wait with knives, bars and bottles but I was like a Honey badger sticking his head in a beehive to rob the honey. The Honey badger gets stung maybe a hundred times but he doesn't give a shit and I was the same. At times I'd be bare knuckle fighting with five men and before I put them to kip I had to take the blows but I didn't give a fuck because my adrenaline was running. Yes I'd have to take a few blows but I was that cranky and hyped up that I wouldn't feel them until the next day anyway.

Lee Duffy used to laugh at me, he'd say, "you're not going to make thirty you ya big bastard but I love ya." Lee told me several times that I had more bottle than anyone he'd ever met and that he respected me.

Now you might not believe this but I'm not a nasty person. I was never like Lee Duffy who could wind people up. Even little Terry Dicko used to wind people up to scare them for the craic. One-time Terry shouted to this innocent bystander, "OI YOU STOLE BRIAN'S PIGEONS" when I was stood there. Obviously the bloke never but he was shitting himself but Terry was just winding him up but I've always been a bit of a people pleaser. Even if it's a joke I don't like people being frightened. I've always craved for people to say, "oh that big Brian's a lovely lad" unless they were scum of the earth or they'd done something to me or my family. I never liked to hear those comments of, "oh Cockerill's massive and I'm shit scared of him!"

When these people wanted to fight me because I had a name I wouldn't just react unless it was personal. Think Manchester United when they were at their best through the 1990s, if South Bank United came out with, "oh we'd play you off the pitch" blah blah blah then Alex Ferguson wouldn't think, I've got to arrange a game with this mob ASAP to teach them all a lesson.

For the record I've always been a fanatical Red Devil because my uncle Frank McGivern played for them. My uncle Frank used to take me to Old Trafford with him when I was younger and I sat with all the players and that's how I became hooked on United.

"THE TAXMAN COMETH."

CHAPTER 16

MENTAL HEALTH & REPENT

These days I work as a care worker and I know what you're thinking, Brian Cockerill doesn't look like your average care worker! Although I don't fit the stereotype in looks it comes very naturally to me. My ex Amanda's sister had her problems I used to help with and so did my brothers Peter and Bobby. I guess you could say it runs in our family because my mam has mental health issues also.

Today in 2020 I'm so glad that people are talking about it much more because many years ago if you had any kind of problems with your mental health you were called a nutter and told to go sign yourself into Lukey's (St Luke's mental hospital in Middlesbrough, now Roseberry Park).

One of the things I'm very good at is studying people and their body language. When I worked the doors I always could read the situation well before anything kicked off. That time Lee Duffy waved me over shouting, "OI OI" then banged me I knew something was wrong, it's just the fucker was that fast and I didn't see it coming (laughs).

I've found with people and mental illness they have certain traits you can read and pick up on. Everyone who's bi-polar do the same things, everybody who's got schizophrenia do the same things. There's psychosis and psychotic people who've brought it on themselves from the alcohol and drugs they've taken which these people should never be looked down upon or frowned at by society.

A girl that I knew, who was a lovely girl was bad and I told her family before she was diagnosed that I believed it was schizophrenia and my comments were met with, "she hasn't got fucking schizophrenia" like it was the end of the world!

I know people frowned upon her like it was leprosy and she needed to be shipped to Australia when in reality it was an illness that couldn't be helped. Myself and someone else took this girl to a doctor on Durham Road in Stockton and there we met a doctor named CJ. What he wanted to do was me to have a conversation with the other person and for me to listen. As I was talking to the other person this doctor came to the side of my face and started whispering into my ear all sorts of rude words to the point that I couldn't even concentrate. When I asked him what he was doing he told me that's exactly what it was like living with schizophrenia and that this lovely girl had voices just like that in her ear. If you can imagine a radio in your ear all day then that's what it's like.

I must admit it was a very unorthodox action from a doctor but after she was seen the doc turned to me and confirmed exactly what I said and she was suffering from schizophrenia.

Today I'm a full-time carer for my brother Bobby who's also had some mental health problems and been sectioned a few times but it's not even a question, I have to be there for my baby brother who's three years younger than me. There's been times when people in authority have tried to put our Bobby in all sorts of units but I've told them "over my fucking dead body!" At times they've tried to keep him in Sandwell House mental hospital in Hartlepool but I've told them firmly Bobby stays with me rather than sit on some ward routinising into space and with vacant thoughts.

The two things none of us can do is live in the past, nor can we live in the future! None of us know if we'll be here tomorrow as that's promised to nobody. All we can do is live for now. When you go to bed on a night and you think of good things then you wake up in the morning happy. If you go to bed bitter, angry and full of venom it carries on the next day. I myself could sit here thinking, oh Amanda left me or why did my ex have to die and life's not fair but I've emptied all that crap out of my mind now. If you allow the issues of life to get on top of you they'll bury you alive like quicksand.

I used to sit there getting stressed out over things like gas bills, everybody gets a gas bill! Everyone in life has these hurdles but if you start getting up in the morning and cracking on then you just get on with it. Forget about stubbing your toe on the table then thinking, oh it's going to be one of them days because that's all bullshit. People getting stressed out because they dropped their phones, it could have happened anytime.

What Brian Cockerill is telling you all to do is look at the glass half-full and not half-empty. Instead of walking around saying nobody cares about you instead say, I'm going to get in that fucking gym today! If you go to the gym you produce endorphins and feel better in your brain. It's the cerebral cortex in your brain which starts getting better which leads to a healthy body healthy mind. With my brother Bobby I cook his breakfast, dinner and tea, wash his clothes, put him in the bath, cut his hair, take him for his injections and medication. It's my duty as his big brother and if tomorrow we were living in a tent then he'd still be there with me along with my dog Scrappy.

Twenty years ago the stuff I do now regarding Bobby wouldn't have entered my head because I was too erratic with what I was doing i.e. fighting and taxing etc, I'd have paid someone else to do it. Today I'm the total opposite to what you saw on Donal Macintyre's Underworld. The way I'm living now I know I'm going to live a lot longer than when I was doing silly shit. These days I'm convinced I'm going to live till I'm 90 because I'm fit, strong and I again have a healthy mind. If anyone's having problems out there then get your head right and the body will follow I promise you.

You couldn't go into a fight thinking, I'm fighting Tyson Fury tomorrow, I might beat him but I'll probably get beat. You just can't do that type of stuff. You must be 100% focused and if you don't really believe you're the best then pretend you are. Be happy and smile because it takes 44 muscles to frown and only 17 to smile so why waste energy! Even if you fake laugh with people you start to feel better inside because your face has changed shape.

Even when I thought I was dying with gallstones and I was rushed into the hospital I forced myself to remain upbeat. North Tees Hospital were unbelievable in looking after me when I had a load of stones removed from my gallbladder. When I was in agony I diagnosed myself and I told them to put me in for an ultrasound which is usually for pregnant women and soft tissues. When I was in that hospital there was six different women who told me it was exactly the same as having a baby because the pains that bad its excruciating and you think you're going to die. I was told that I could have quite possibly brought it on myself when I used to drink ten pints of milk a day.

The biggest thing about myself is helping people and always has been.

Many years ago when I was with Amanda our Jordan came in the house and told me there was this 13-year-old kid who was now homeless. He said his mam had flung him out and now he was sleeping on a field so I told Jordan to get him fucking round here now! When he came around he was 6ft tall which was incredible considering his age. Incidentally it was Ryan the kid from the Macintyre documentary. As soon as Ryan came in my house I took to him right away. For the next five years Ryan was in and out of my house and now he's on the straight path doing well and very much totally alive. There was also another kid named Chris who lived around the corner from me with his mam. Chris and his family were having all sorts of problems but our Jordan came in one day and asked me, "dad can he stay here" which I agreed to. He went on to live with us for eighteen months. Many times the social workers would come and vet my house and I'd get their full support. Another kid who Jordan brought home was when this kid came into ours and he was having problems at home. What was happening was his dad was in the SAS and he wanted his boy to be tough like him but it just wasn't in the lad. Anyway the dad ended up being a fucking bully towards the boy. I didn't like that but I never got involved, that was until the dad punched this little skinny kid and gave him a great big black eye so I took him in. He stayed at ours and I would give this kid a cuddle and showed him some love. I had that boy in our house for three weeks and never once did we have any trouble with him.

There used to be a probation officer named Derek who used to come to my house to keep in contact with all these strays I used to adopt. He told me that considering all that he'd heard about Brian Cockerill was that he was evil that I was actually a lovely man.

Derek used to insist that all these kids came to the Cockerill Inn. Over the years loads of kids came to stay at my house when they had nowhere in the world to go and I would sit and talk to these kids. Sometimes, where I live in Ingleby Barwick, Jordan would bring maybe twenty to thirty kids ranging from 12 to 15 years old and they'd all sit in my front garden wanting me to tell them stories. Most of them wanted to know about fighting but I wouldn't talk on that side. I'd tell them they should only copy me in the training department. One night, I'm not kidding you, me and Amanda had seven different kids staying who needed a roof over their heads. We even had a little three-year old staying and when he left he was crying saying he wanted to stay with Brian with muscles forever.

Many years later after I looked after this one kid, I was in a shop when this big lad was really staring at me to the point I was getting uncomfortable and thought he was going to have a go at me, that was until he said, "Brian it's me Chris." Then I twigged, it was the lad who'd stayed at my house for 18 months. He told me how he remembered that I looked after him and that I told him to become an electrician but he'd become a plumber instead. He told me how he now has a little daughter and just that he wanted to thank me from the bottom of his heart and that I saved his life. Ryan was the same and he's doing really well in life in London working. He's now married with kids so it makes it all worthwhile when I hear the stories like that but I never did it for any thanks.

There were also times I talked people out of hanging themselves and I would go and meet all these different types of people because it gave them encouragement because they said they'd heard about this big Brian Cockerill as if I was some sort of legend. I know it's far from the truth but this is what these kids saw in their eyes when they met me. I never said no to any of these troubled souls by the way as it was the least I could do.

Many times I have written down diets for people like I was a doctor handing out prescriptions. I would bray it into them not for them to let me down and that I was proud of them. Maybe the best thing I've ever done in my entire existence was when I saved a little boy's life on Redcar sea front. There was a little boy on his bike around maybe 5 years old and he was on a bike and he went out in front of a van, I saw this and immediately fucking ran and grabbed him, obviously taking him off his feet, the van must have missed me by inches. At the last second his mam saw what was going down and she screamed in sheer agony thinking her boy was gone but I got there in time. I screamed at the man driving in the van what the fuck was he playing at and he was really shaken up because he knew just how close he'd come to wiping that kid out for good.

Another time I was with my brother Skinny up Gypsy Lane in Nunthorpe when we saw this bloke driving all over. I thought that bastards pissed so we followed him near Nunthorpe train crossing and we were trying to ram him off the road to save people's lives when it turns out he was slumped at the wheel. I managed to catch up with his car and as I opened the car door I went to punch him in the face when I realised he was out cold. It turns out he hadn't had his insulin injection and blacked out at the wheel. If he'd have been in a normal car it would have conked out but because he was in an automatic the car kept going with his foot on the pedal. When my mates the boys in blue arrived they couldn't believe that Brian Cockerill had just done some good.

One of the biggest things for me in doing this book with Jamie Boyle and the other bits and pieces we're going to be doing is to let people know that that book by Steve Richards wasn't the real Brian Cockerill. All he wanted to talk about was fighting and taxing but there's a much bigger side to me than just that person. I'm only glad after more than 13 years I can finally set the record straight at last because I don't like people being scared of me before they even know me. Today if you see Brian Cockerill in the street than please come and give me a hug and I'll know exactly why you've done it, because you've read this book.

"Never interrupt your enemy whilst he's making a mistake."

Napoleon Bonaparte

CHAPTER 17

RAOUL THE COWARD

I was pretty vocal in The Evening Gazette in 2014 and on a documentary which was named Dispatches which aired on the BBC. The show asked me my views on murderous gunman Raoul Moat. The truth is I'd never met Moat but we moved in similar social circles and I knew people from jail who knew him very well. The BBC themselves sort of skimmed over my real thoughts because what I really said was Northumbria police were more at fault than what was put in the media.

When Raoul was phoning his girlfriend Samantha up threatening to kill her, the prison services knew about it then they told the police. What really should have happened to a ticking timebomb like him was for him to have been gate arrested at Durham nick and it would have saved a hell of a lot of misery as well as lives. I said on Dispatches that the authorities need to only look at the number of lives and casualties to make sure that there's never another Raoul Moat that walks out of those prison gates when they're clearly not ready to be let back into society. That man was more of a danger than he was ten weeks earlier when he was first put in.

It does really bug me when there's people out there inside of prison or in society who are committing crime using my name saying I'm behind it all when really I haven't a Scooby-Doo what these people are up to let alone making little bundles of fortunes from their criminal activities.

Another thing that happens in Middlesbrough often is the old, "I'm going to get Brian Cockerill on to you" and it's just for the worst kind of narcotics there is out there that exist. I've actually been out drinking in Middlesbrough town centre when I've had thrown at me, "ERE YOU YA DAFT CUNT I'M GONNA GET BRIAN COCKERILL ON TO SORT YOU IN THE MORNING!"

I've lost count of how many times I've walked into a licenced establishment when one of the doormen will march over to tell me, "your sisters just been in Bri but don't worry I looked after her." Then I've had to tell him that my sister is abroad. In Teesside I must have eighteen sisters, ten brothers, god knows how many nephews, nieces, mam's, dads and god knows what else.

Say for instance Tommy Smith was going to someone's house, it wouldn't be put on Facebook but if I have done its put on. Even if I'm just sat minding my own business or having a kebab at Teesside Park whoever is sat next to me takes sneaky photos and it goes on social media at some point so that's why I could never be a bank robber anymore because I'm too well known and everybody knows me, even if they really don't if you know what I mean!

When I was running my Cockerill Security business I thought it was other rival companies pinching my signs when really as I've already told you it was these young kids using them as posters for their bedroom or there mam and dad's sheds. When it was first happening I was getting dead paranoid and I was thinking about how I was going to walk into their office and massacre whoever it was. If you're reading this kids and you continually stole my security protection business badges for years then you'll never have any idea just how much you almost made some business owner pay. In the end and after a lot of extensive investigating I found out it was a group of lads in their late teens from over the border then bragging that they've got Brian Cockerill's company looking after their uncle Harry's, Rodney's cousin's budgies premises. That just shows how big my name was.

My philosophy is Brian Cockerill doesn't believe you should ever hit a minor. I've even had young fearless kids trying it on who are maybe Featherweights dripping wet like the one time I was in The Powerhouse in Redcar. The place was just a rave club on Redcar sea front. It was that hot that everyone used to walk around with the sweat dripping off the ceiling. Anyway, this tall drip of a lad pushed by everyone in my full view and at the same time he was telling people he was this superstar British Army boxing champion. This beanpole of a lad was really giving it "the big un" to anyone who'd listen but at that exact moment and lucky for him I was already on three different charges, one more and I'd have been in jail. Anyway for some reason he shouted over to me that he knew he could beat me in a fight blah blah blah… I still said nothing but my mates Goosey and Mally who's not long recently passed away had both told him not to be so fucking stupid and asked if he had a death wish or was it the drugs that he was on?! Well this big skinny mouthpiece kept going on and on so the other thing apart from batter him I could do was to buy him a drink. Well before he got better he got worse and no he still reckons that I was terrified of him and that I'm trying to buy his lordship's friendship and now he was really annoying me so I've told him to fuck off and now I don't even want to be his friend so just fuck the fuck off away from me. Peter Hoe and his wife were watching all that was going down with the world's biggest arsehole. Honest to god I was going to leave this dick alone and I'd done well to all night but when I watched him get into a fighting stance with his feet it was blatantly obvious what he was about to do to me so I walloped him with lightning speed and he was out cold for maybe 4-5 minutes. When he woke up the doormen put him out because they'd seen the way he'd been going on. As he was being carried out I thought, you weren't that much of a fucking tester because that's one of the things he said that he was. That only happened because my name was Brian Cockerill and another well-known Middlesbrough man was there with a rep as big as mine, it was Eston's Peter Hoe. To be honest I'd gotten past it and he was winding me up that much that I didn't even care about going to prison.

Another fella who was the same as that fella and had a name was called Micky. One night I was in the old Middlesbrough nightclub Blaises when all of a sudden Micky walked up to me, stared then shouted, "WHO YOU LOOKING AT?" I turned around and there was nobody there apart from little Kev Auer (God rest him) then he went to attack me. I couldn't believe it I was in shock but also I was fuming. In the end I've hit him that hard that his cheekbone went through his nose. There was something wrong with his eye socket also.

After that incident that's when I really started becoming scared of what I was capable of. I know for it to be 100% true that Micky was told that if that blow had been one more inch to the side I'd have killed him. Sadly Micky went on to get stabbed to death in March 2001 at a family friends barbeque. Kevin Auer told me afterwards, he said, "Brian these people only want to fight you so they can say they've been game enough to have a fight with Scotch Bri!" Micky and his brother Paul were once top boxers. Kev Auer told me afterwards, "Brian you didn't just beat him you fucking annihilated him" and trust me Kevin Auer could really fight for fun. When Micky's brother Paul found out about his brother I heard he was screaming saying, "who's done this to you, I'll fucking kill them?" Then when he was told it was Cockerill I heard he calmed down considerably and he was said to have been heard to say, "well I bet you asked for it!"

Another night I was coming out of The Madison in Newcastle with Stephen & Michael Sayers when there was this guy and he was shouting to everyone just how much he was the top international boxer in England. Straight away the Sayers brothers could see him working away with anyone who was there. A lot of them just let it go because fighting isn't everyone's thing is it, plus it was very visible on the eye that this guy could have a row. In the end I think this loudmouth must have started pissing off Stephen and Michael because they both made it clear to me that this fella had no serious links to them. That's when I told him calmly to wrap it in the way he was going on or he was going to get it. Well he didn't take kindly to my friendly word and with that he lunged for me and then I've slapped him and knocked him clean out with a slap. There was a lot of people in Tyneside who witnessed that and what really went down including the Sayers family.

These days I would much rather sit somebody down and try to talk sense into these hungry and up and coming lions. Today there's lots of new Lee Duffy's out there and their paths have already been chosen for them. The path that they have chosen has yet to break their mothers hearts. When I think of young impressionable kids I think of Christopher Crossan (Bram) who's ambition in life was to be me when he was older. I'm glad to report that Bram's now found god but before he found god he would be constantly looking for me to ask about training or diets. I've never worried about maybe giving one of these young pups too much information and then they look for me all big and strong to come and turn on me. Maybe he was more than capable of doing exactly that put thankfully he's not that type of lad.

Another lad named Mark Owens was a professional boxer he's the lad who had my signature tattooed on him. Mark was only boxing a journeyman type but he became a world champion as a kickboxer.

Eric "The Viking" Thompson was another I've spent a bit of time training with and is Mark's mate from Sunderland. I'll train anyone but only if you never mistreat the training and discipline I show you. There's nothing worse than getting caught out in a situation with some big name in a fight and you haven't trained. It's not all about fighting though, it's just great to be fight-fit isn't it people?! If I ever found out that a person I've been training has been bullying people it's over for me for life.

Some people still use my name and they have even done it while this book has been written. I suppose the life I've led and even the stuff I've never done I've got to be dragged down and be accounted for. Its karma isn't it and I believe it all evens itself out in the end.

I'll tell you one story, there was this one night I was on a gypsy camp and there was a lot of well-known criminal faces that the police may have been interested in. We were just there to watch a bareknuckle fight and there was 180 in total watching. Then the police helicopter was heard but out of every face that was there the police helicopter followed me home and no one else.

What I would like to finish this chapter on though is if ever you're threatened by Brian Cockerill's name I can promise you I'm not behind it. In fact if someone says that they're going to get Brian Cockerill on to you then double bluff them and say, "oh I've got Brian's number I'll ring him and ask him now" and watch how their body language changes.

If it's you using my name then please give it a rest and let an old man enjoy his twilight years. I've seen the inside of police cells far too much so PLEASE let me enjoy what's left no matter how funny it is or how much you'll put the shits up so-so by doing it. If it's a genuine reason then contact me via Facebook though. Although there's been some funny ones there's been some terrible ones like people saying I was going to do all sorts to people. One day this person started crying saying to me, "oh please don't burn my house down Brian!" When I've asked him what the hell he was on about he said people had been using my name to do all sorts which wasn't anything to do with me. Terry Dicko is the worst of them all because he winds people up that I'm going to be doing everything but it's just a big laugh to Terry.

I'll tell you one thing on what people have started to do because the Brian Cockerill brand got so big was folk were getting drugs or large amounts of cigarettes off Big Bri but they weren't, so then what they were doing was going back to their best mates or gang members and just saying, "that cunt Brian Cockerill has taxed me" knowing full-well that nobody would come after me and they'd get away with the debt. There was one man I found pulling this scam in Blackhall so I went up there with Vulture, Robbie Lancaster and my brother Jamie had come with us. In fact Terry and Kev Richardson also came, who were top fighters from Hartlepool, I mean, the latter used to spar with my old mate

Dave Garside. Anyway, when I got to the bottom of what he was saying, he was telling everyone that I'd stolen £20,000 off him which was a complete and utter pack of lies. I was that mad that this bloke had made up this tall story that he had two British Bulldogs and I stole them both, the dogs were worth £3,000 each. I know you might think I was out of order but who the fuck does this guy think he is to make up stories from nowhere saying I've terrorised him and his family when it was all utter nonsense. The fact of the matter is I could have been shot and killed for something I hadn't even done which is scary when you strip it right down.

That's happened a few times were people have said, "oh Brian Cockerill's just robbed two ounces of crack cocaine" so they've just left it and the debts been buried. I'll never forget Terry Richardson saying to me once, have you just taxed the shop Tin-Pan Alley which was a shop on Stockton High Street". I never answered him but then he went on to tell me that this shop were bragging to Terry saying I'd done whatever and using my name as if it was an honour that I'd just been in and taxed them like it was something to brag about. I didn't admit anything but Terry said, "I don't know a man in the country who can get away with doing what you do Brian."

"Brian Cockerill was one powerful man who oozed politeness and manners. Brian treat everybody with respect and if anyone says otherwise then they've never met the real Brian Cockerill."

Manny Burgo Jnr
Ex-professional heavyweight boxer

CHAPTER 18

TEESSIDE'S SEEDY WORLD

If you read this book and you think I fucking hate the police then believe me mate you've got that wrong. What I do hate is when the police abuse their authorities so I refuse to let them get away with it like the time me and Paddy Watson (Woga) pulled the police up for speeding. Woga is no longer here now but to put it bluntly the guy was a loose cannon. He ended his life in Cargo Fleet House in September 2001, I think it was Jamie Boyle's dad who found him, as he was the concierge in there. Towards the end of his time he was on the run and staying in safe houses in places such as Hartlepool, Doncaster and even down South where he shacked up with one of the Richardson family until he pushed her out of the window. The last time I ever saw Woga was at the Mike Tyson V Julius Francis fight in Manchester in January 2000. Now Woga wasn't what you would call a hardcase but he definitely lived in that villainy world. I'll never forget it was Woga who rang me and said, "Bri have a look outside your front window there's a man watching you and that's the regional crime squad and they've called it "operation gorilla" and he was right. After Woga's advice I then stayed in the house for ten days.` I bet you're asking why they called putting me away, "operation gorilla" well why do you think (laughs) the cheeky bastards! Operations cost thousands and thousands of pounds to put in place and I didn't even get a banana out of it! Jokes aside I'd love to know the hundreds of thousands of pounds the police have spent to put me away when all they've ever gotten me for is driving offences. Al Capone was done by the Chicago police in the end and went away on tax evasion charges because that's all they could get him on.

I would get the police attention day and night even when I was out taking the dog for a walk or just taking the wife to Tesco's so I did used to snap at them and get ratty with them. One day me and Speedy (Mark Hornsby who went on to be murdered by Boola) started following this car who'd been following me all day so I started following him. Anyway after about fifteen minutes a half a dozen of his mates turned up and when they got close to me they asked me what I was doing. I just said, "now it's your turn TIG" and drove off.

One day I was in Leeds and I found a tracking device on the bottom of my car which was as big as a mobile phone by the way and worth about 30K. I took it to Kevin Kilty's brother to find out what it was because he was in the forces. I was told that the bug had a frequency which was on for ten seconds and then going off for two seconds. This bug was top of the range and only used by the likes of MI5. When I eventually took the battery out at Teesside Park you should have seen the armed response fly out in their numbers, the person who was with me counted 17-armed response were there to take me away because at that time I was huge. As this was going on I was allowed a call to my solicitors Watson & Woodhouse. Good old Jimmy Watson was the best of the best in his field and shrewder than the criminals he represented. The man knew what he was doing in criminal law and that's why every bad guy in the Boro went to him to get him off. To give you an example just how good Jimmy Watson was it was he who got Davey Allo off from doing a life sentence over murdering Lee Duffy and BamBam allegedly shooting Kev Hawkes so he had real calibre for the Middlesbrough underworld cases. I'm not going to go into it but if it wasn't for Jimmy Watson I'd have given Charles Bronson a run for his money in the years he's clocked up in all them CAT A nicks around England.

In life you get good baddies like myself i.e. would never hurt woman and children etc then you get bad goodies and I'll tell you one story of one of my friends from Leeds named Rudy X. Now Rudy was very familiar in Middlesbrough and as game as they came. Rudy died going to see his dad on his death bed for the last time. Then on the way home to Middlesbrough it was alleged he was rammed off the road by Middlesbrough police so the week after Rudy's poor mother had to bury her husband and her son at the same time. I know a lot more of the ins and outs of that case but legally I'd better not say anymore.

One-time Rudy had a pub in Parkend named The Newmarket and was one dangerous man. When I got out of jail in 1996 he was running the town himself and was extremely close with the notorious Clifton Bryan. I eventually ended up taxing Rudy and not long after he turned up at Club M (Yarm) and I told Rudy if he or his twelve mates wanted a go then I'd step outside with any of them. I told Rudy that Middlesbrough was my fucking town and I don't go to Leeds doing things I shouldn't so I basically told him to fuck right off and I took another 3K worth of gear off him, I was with Malcolm Lea (Flee) It was alleged that Rudy and Clifton spent 20% of their income on major artillery which proves that both were dangerous dangerous people. I had nothing to do with Clifton Bryan's death but it was alleged that I had. What linked me with the Leed's man Clifton Bryan was I'd started buying the crack at a really low price which couldn't be matched. It turns out that Clifton Bryan was shot over a measly ten grand and was buried in a glass coffin in January 2002. The sad thing is Clifton was over Manchester way doing his dealing when he had a young kid who wasn't even from that world in the car so he copped it and lost his life also. It just shows you doesn't it that death respects no one and with that kid he was just in the wrong place at the wrong time.

Going back to me and my own police harassment, what I would do was sit outside of Middlesbrough's then police HQ and take all their numbers. If I was ever chased I was never caught. Also my argument if I was being caught was, because there's so many Osman warnings on my life and I'm being followed night and day, isn't it my right to know who is and who isn't a copper when my life is at risk.

Sometimes I would be talking to the police but I'd be that on edge thinking they weren't police and they were really crims and had come to whack me the Chicago mafia style like Capones men did on 14th February 1929, its why it's known as The Saint Valentine's Day Massacre, it took place in the exact same fashion. It's believed that mob boss Al Capone had seven of his enemies kidnapped by a team all dressed in police uniforms and placed against a wall in a dark alley. Only these weren't officers of the law but Capones men and I often thought that was going to happen to me. Sometimes a police officer may be talking to me quite civilly but at the same time I'd be saying to him, "GET YA

FUCKING HANDS ON THE CAR SO I CAN SEE EM YOU". Sometimes if I knew they were a rat I'd talk to them like utter shit, I'm not joking. How bad I talked to them depended on just how deep I knew into their personal lives.

Often the police would want to arrest me for jaywalking across a road but I'd make a point of finding out about my rivals. Sometimes I knew their daughters would be pilling it at the weekend on the local rave scene because she'd be purchasing from friends of mine, so I'd always make them know little things like that if it became personal between us. You needed as much ammo if it was an all-out game of cat & mouse i.e. kill or be killed! The one thing I was very aware of is I'd learn from other people's mistakes i.e. did he get caught with money and gear together, etc, etc... As you get older your criminal brain becomes much wiser and if you're lucky you learn quickly otherwise it will take a lot of years off your life. When I was going on jobs I'd often think about if I were a police officer, how would I catch myself? Then I'd answer my own question "with a bug!"

Truth be known I've always been switched on since I was a kid, one of my biggest fears was that my own crimes wouldn't put me away but that I'd be put away for a long time by being framed. Several times I threatened officers before they searched my vehicles I'd say, "ere you dirty bastard If you fit anything in any of my cars I'll actually have you shot. Mark my words if it's the last thing I do I'd actually have you executed!" I was always told that they wouldn't dream of doing such a thing but it was a huge fear of mine for years. It was always in the back of my mind just how dirty and corrupt Cleveland police were and for them I was their jewel in their crown, the apple in the pig's mouth. Another thing I pointed out to the head police officer was that when they bugged my car I took the registration off the bug and kept it, if they didn't bug my car then why would I have the serial number of that bug? By law your supposed to have Home Office approvement permission to do this and they didn't. I could tell they were flapping when their reply was, "aah ya not going to make a statement against us are ya Brian because we could lose our job's over this?" One of them even said, "we've been left with egg on our faces" but I told him it was more like a full English. Kevin Kilty was there that day with me to prove I'm telling the truth.

One of the most comical police raids was when one of the doughnuts ran in shouting, "BINGO! BINGO GUVNOR!", obviously they thought it was one of the biggest bags of cocaine they'd ever seen, that was until they smelt a little bit and realised it was just a big bag of artex, the daft cunts! A few of my mates have asked me if I did that on purpose because I was so well watched by the police, but as much as I'd like to say yes I didn't. They're just thick as fuck!

Some nights in the early 90's I would listen to them on the scanner talking and saying things about me like, "target one is moving" then straight away I would turn to my mates saying, "OI OI that's me." Then they're saying things like, "target two's with him (Smally)" and "we've got the armed response ready coming from Morpeth."

Straight away I rang my old solicitor Craig Bier and I said that a friend of mine has just been listening to the local scanners and apparently he's heard there's an armed response team coming looking for me with loaded guns and I'm really frightened. Craig then rang the police and relayed what I'd heard and added that, "it's not Brian Cockerill that you should be looking for."

It's funny because when he started talking again on the radio (which he knew that people were listening on) he said it's no longer target one, meaning that whoever the gobshite is has aborted the whole project and it's now completely fucked. In fact after Craig Bier rang up the copper on the scanner said, "it's not Brian Cockerill is it Brian? but we know you're out there listening to everything that we're saying. "

If you want the truth (which this book is 100% about) that I've had some hostile moments with police let me tell you about one evening when I had just finished on Stockton High Street. Addish and Mark Johnson used to run The Mall door and most weekends when we finished together we would always go for something to eat in Middlesbrough which was about four miles away. As we got to Middlesbrough town centre around 11pm (before we went to get the takeaway) Addish started looking into this place on Linthorpe Road which sold three piece suits, but as he was peering into the shop at this amazing sale two awful police officers with appalling attitudes jumped out shouting, "WHAT THE FUCK YOU TWO DOING?" it was because Addish and Mark were two black lads you see.

That's when I very civilly intervened and I told them that they weren't doing anything and that they were just looking and having a nosey but this rude officer told me he believed otherwise. Even though this officer had no proof he wanted all of our names, but I'm in no mood so I tell him to piss off and that he's not getting my name and address. I told the officer that the only reason that he was kicking off is because he was trying to pick on Addish and Mark because they were black when all of a sudden this mini Hitler radioed in, "I NEED BACK UP URGENTLY!" Well you can guess what happens next. Three police vans and around eight officers all turned up demanding that I walk into the birdcage and they were the cat, well I was in no fucking mood so I told them all I hadn't done anything and that all I wanted to do was to eat my kebab which was on order, the police then switch methods and try to be my best mates.

This must have been around 1990 when I'd had my wrangle with The Duffer and I was fucking massive, I was easily 23st plus and so irate because I hadn't done anything and I was fucking starving, but I ended up in the back of the van as they asked. I thought I hadn't done anything so I'm going to be the model citizen. That was until I heard the coppers in the front blatantly yelling fucking lies about me saying I'd done this, that and the other. Well this really put me on one and I'm not going to lie, not only was I fucking fuming but now I had fully blown roid rage and I barged into the back of the copper van door, 'BANG!' the back doors flew open. The police who I see then look at each other as if to say, 'he's broke the fucking door so let's all run like Godzilla was on the loose.' Then before you could even blink there was another set of around twenty police and to look at the scene you'd think it was from a fucking mass murder. Luckily for me this was in the days before the CS gas as no doubt I'd have been taken down from it being plastered in my face.

I think for a couple of minutes that the police didn't know what to do with me, for a start the coppers started bickering between themselves like, "you get in the back with him" then it was only being met with a reply from a few others saying, "NAAH FUCK OFF I'M NOT GETTING IN THE BACK WITH HIM" and it went on like that for maybe a few minutes. I'll never forget that one of the female officers described me as a, "wild untamed Silverback Gorilla" which made me laugh and maybe it's where the name came from a few years later when they tried to put me away for good with 'Operation Gorilla.' Afterwards the police were quizzing me on just how I snapped the door and I told them it was an accident. I told them I just ran at them and half-heartedly done it and their response was, "that's unbelievable."

One other scenario was when I was in Silks Nightclub in Redcar and there had been a load of trouble, at the time I didn't know that Silks had been taken over by new management so as I was walking in I was told, "you're going to have to pay mate", but I told him, "I don't have to pay." Anyway before anything else was said I knocked four of the doormen out and they phoned the police. I would say this was around 1993/94 but this top DCI came on his own for some reason, he introduced himself as DCI so-so and told me that outside he had eleven officers but I needed to calm down and everything would be ok. He also half threatened me by telling me that the rest of the Redcar constabulary were only seconds away so I needed to calm down. At that point Roy Morley walked past (who used to have the Hydro) and he said that he'd walked past and it was like a scene from Cagney & Lacey, me alone being hunted down.

Roy said there was blue flashing lights everywhere and that you'd think that there had been a mass murder where we were. Anyway as the police were negotiating with me and the club owners I told the club owners that if I have to leave this club it will be the worst thing to ever happen to their club. I told him I had fifty lads all in that club at that exact night all monitoring the situation extremely closely. In the end the manager told the police that I hadn't done anything and that I was welcome to stay.

To be honest I only stayed for twenty minutes or so because I was too wound up so I decided I wanted to go somewhere else. On the way downstairs I observed around eight police officers and again I walked up to the lot of them closely observing them telling each and every officer that he needed a shave, or he needed to polish his shoes. My parting words to them were, "CARRY ON SOLDIERS!" And that was that!

You know one time I was pulled over doing 32mph in a 30mph zone, when I pulled over the police officer told me he wasn't bothered about me speeding but he thought I was banned so he was going to have to take me in and I said, "no problem officer" which totally threw him. "Really?" he replied and I gave him my word. I think he even thought, hang on, here's me 5ft 4, 10st , with no tanks, CS spray, guns, SAS, taking Brian Cockerill in. He later told me he felt dead chuffed.

When we walk inside the Middlesbrough custody suite I could see all the other shift looking at him thinking what the fuck? And you know what the reason behind that all was? He was polite beyond his means! If he would have come over thirty handed and started pushing me about then he would have met a very different Mr Cockerill. In the end I shook that officers hand in front of the full station and I said, "if the whole of Cleveland police force were like you then Teesside would be a better place."

The screws in Durham and Holme House were the same and I told them all to be polite to me if they wanted anything. The sad thing was for me in prison was that I couldn't get a job because if I kicked off nobody could handle me. Mr Davison was really trying to vouch for me but I understood the prison procedure. In fact one of the screws in there got the sack because he gave me a couple of stamps when he wasn't supposed to which I found fucking scandalous and of course terrible.

"The eyes are the windows to the soul."

William Shakespeare

CHAPTER 19

TRUE CRIME TODAY

Crime today in Britain has gone through the roof and has witnessed exponential growth. A lot of these rappers are responsible for the way the youth are today. I mean all they seem to rap about is putting caps in people's arses or blowing people away so violence is more socially accepted than ever before. In my era you had singers like Blondie and Jimmy Somerville singing about love whereas now the younger generation have got daft rappers with jeans down their arses rapping about their mates being blown away or what jail was like.

In 2020 I don't care what you fucking say, kids are out there on the streets carrying knives for fun. I mean I read a status the other day that Grangetown in Middlesbrough has pound for pound more people murdered than anywhere else in Europe. I think it was around double figures and then you've got the areas such as Eston and Stockton where the crime rates are increasing horrifically. Most of the crimes today are to do with drugs for example with 'blues' (otherwise known as Valium) which usually aren't even the real things, people are taking these things and blacking out then going out and murdering people purely due to being on them. What happens when you take these things is even though your mind switches off and the lights shall we say go out, your body has a natural instinct to survive.

I was in jail with one kid and he'd shot a hole through a taxi door, then went in to kill his girlfriend and he didn't know anything about it for three days because he'd had thirty blues. There's another one on Teesside named Neil Maxwell from Benefit Street who'd killed someone on them tablets. When he came around he couldn't remember killing someone in broad daylight but a minimum term of 30 years soon brought him back to reality as that kid will be at least seventy before he's even up for parole.

I believe that these kids on Teesside are seeing these daft rappers or the films and wanting to show off themselves by carrying these evil looking tools around, maybe even just for show but I guarantee that if they were being beat up in a scuffle it's the first thing they'd use. Can you imagine being bullied and the only way you could defend yourself was to use this knife that you were carrying? The courts wouldn't understand that it was the other party that started on you, they'd just see a cold-blooded murderer stood in the dock with several decades of prison to go with it. When I was a kid we'd go out playing 'kick the can' or just footy in general, whereas these days you see 12-year olds smoking joints, walking down the streets on mobile phones watching people getting their heads cut off and porn, and if that wasn't gruesome enough they share them on to their mates.

The likes of Lee Duffy from 1990/91 wouldn't have lasted as long doing what he did back then in this day and age. Today you can be talking to a normal person who can't fight but because he's been smoking crack all night it gives him that sense of no-fear and paranoia all rolled into one. I think that's a lot to do with these lunatics carrying weapons. Years ago when me and Duffy were at it occasionally there were weapons but not like there is today.

Every single weekend in Middlesbrough someone is getting knifed or slashed and it just seems to be the norm. Many years ago when the armed response were out it was usually for Brian Cockerill, now they're out for fun which is a good thing because it protects us from all these acts of terrorism. Truth be told and I'm not trying to be clever but it was me who stopped the guns coming up to Teesside through the 1980s.

I won't name them but it was lads trying to ship them through from London, Manchester, Liverpool and Newcastle but I put a stop to it. I wouldn't let guns inside Middlesbrough. These days in Middlesbrough there's guns on the street but it's nowhere near the level of Manchester and Liverpool because down there there's a gun in every three streets I'm telling you! The gun crime for the North West is staggering and doing an armed robbery is the most popular crime. In Middlesbrough the knife crime is particularly bad because you can find a knife anywhere. For instance, you can nick a knife from your mam's draw. These kids walk around Middlesbrough with a 10-inch blade and I say to them, "it's not to peel potatoes is it?"

I'll never forget I went over to Hartlepool to tax these drug dealers who are all in jail now. It was near Rossmere Park and as I went to the house I thought right, I'm going to make a bucketful of money here. I knocked on the door but they obviously never answered because they'll have seen my large frame through the glass door, I went around the side of the house when I clocked one of the dealers going to make a run for it. Instantly I shout his name but he runs back in the house, within seconds he comes back out holding a gun so I ran at him and he fucking shot me in the stomach. I looked down thinking I was going to see my insides hanging out but it was one of them daft yellow BB pellets. He'd shot me with a BB gun but that just made me angrier. Lucky for him I left it as I saw two little toddlers playing in the back garden so I left it and walked away. A little while later I got a call from Mr 007 BB shooter and he said he now wanted to fight me with all his crew which he had all inside his vehicle with him.

It must have been a big car as he said there was seventeen there with him. He was either lying or he was in one of them tanks you see on The A-Team. Anyway the next day again I arranged to fight the lot of them one after the other, I took Richy Horsley and a few others just to make sure I wasn't going to be gunned down, it was all arranged that we were going to fight outside The Lagoon which is near Seaton Carew but again they never turned up. They all bottled it.

As I've said somewhere in this book, Teesside is the worst place for knife crime in the country and trust me I've been reading up on the figures, this is why in 2020 with the platform Jamie Boyle has given me I want to get out there to the schools, prisons and youth clubs and advise these kids to run like fuck away from that life. What these kids are doing, the crimes they are committing aren't human and its damn right animalistic and I'm begging to be given a chance to get out on the streets of Middlesbrough and help put a stop to this. I'm not saying I'm better than the police but what I am saying is I know the streets and I lived that life for over thirty years. I know how it all works and I know how these kids think because once upon a time l was just one of them too.

For some reason though, God didn't hand me the same fate as Lee Duffy, Tommy, Robbie & Peter Hoe, Speedy, Boola, Viv Graham, Harry Lancaster, Mark Sayers, Paddy Watson, Kev Auer, John MacPartland, John McCormack, Keith McQuade and Paul Debrick and I didn't end up doing a life sentence like Paul Bryan or Gary Vinter, so I believe him upstairs has given me my biggest vocation to date yet and that's to change Middlesbrough.

A little story about one of the names above, Gary Vinter, who's now serving a whole life tariff for double murder. Gary was originally from Grangetown/Eston way and around 6ft 6 and 20st plus. One day he was having a few issues with a group of lads in Boro, funnily enough it was my friend Sean's cousins but I sorted it all out for him. I became quite 'pally' you could say with Vinter but he was a bully with it and as I got to know him more and more I didn't like him. The piece of shit went on to take two lives over a decade apart, one poor lass he stabbed to death around fifty times, God rest her. In the end because of his bullying ways I ended up putting it on Vinter's toes and surprisingly he met fire with fire and told me he wanted to come to Ingleby Barwick to have a one on one.

Vinter told me he wanted to meet me at the back of Tesco's in Ingleby Barwick, he also told me to be ready because he was bringing a knife. By that point I was fucking blowing fire and I told him to bring a tank and the British Army because I'm going to pull his fucking head right off. Anyway a good few hours go by and I'm getting ready to go and bury this big dopey daft shithouse when my Mrs got a call from him saying, "Amanda it's me Gary, I'm hiding at the moment in Eston cemetery shitting myself and I daren't go home because Brian's going to kill me." He was basically begging for Amanda to call me off if you like, the big coward. You know when you mention the name Gary Vinter it angers me because he wasn't right, he'd already been put away for murder then was let out to kill again which the authorities need to hold their hands up to.

Today he's still at it inside, he was the one who took that beast Roy Whiting's eye out in 2011 saying, "that's the monster who killed the little girl Sarah Payne" so Vinter should probably have been given a medal for that. Talking about Vinter's murderous rampage he killed his work colleague Carl Edon, 22, and received a life sentence with a 10-year minimum term in 1996. He was freed in 2005 but was recalled to his life sentence for his part in a pub brawl in Eston on New Year's Eve 2006. Now the reason I've even included that piece of shit Vinter in this book so much was the story of the first person who Vinter killed Carl Edon. Carl was from Middlesbrough but from the age of five told both his parents that he was the reincarnation of a German soldier from the second world war.

Carl's parents brought him up hearing this story for all of his life and to be honest they must have thought he had mental health issues. Carl would often tell his parents that he was a German bomber in the war and he died and was blown up not far from where Gary Vinter went on to kill him. Now I know you might be reading this and thinking, ooh Brian's back on the gear again but if you Google Carl Edon/Gary Vinter German bomber reincarnation you can read it for yourself and what will even blow you away more is the picture of the German bomber is the spitting image of Carl Edon. I couldn't possibly put into writing the similarities so please check it out on the internet.

I know even when I was telling the author Jamie Boyle for this book he was looking at me funny as if, 'Brian what the fuck are you talking about you crazy bastard' but please Google what I've just relayed to you all. The German bomber and Carl Edon were both killed around the same place even though one was from Germany and one was from Middlesbrough. In fact when little Carl Edon was growing up he told people he lost his leg and was badly burnt in his past life as a German bomber. Well when Carl Edon was born he had a huge birthmark at the top of his leg. Two years after Carl was murdered the wreckage of a German Bomber plane was found buried just off Tilbury Road in South Bank only a few hundred yards from the spot where Carl was killed. When the bomber was dug up the German bomber pilots remains where still inside. During the excavation it was discovered that the pilots leg had been severed in the wreckage as Carl had said. When the pilot was buried in Thornaby Carl's parents attended the funeral.

It all never made sense to poor Carl's parents until after his death when all the pieces of the jigsaw were put together by television programmes and papers etc… You just couldn't make that up!

"I was introduced to Brian Cockerill by Lee Duffy. Lee actually told me in his own words that Brian was the hardest man he'd ever come across in his life. The fact is Brian was a special fighter and on his day nobody would have even come close to beating him."

Stephen Sayers

CHAPTER 20

PLEASE GOD FORGIVE ME

I'm going to be brutally honest with you and tell you all now, my past is a load of shit! My god how do I regret the full lot of it. Today in 2020 I'm 55 and if God spares me, I'd like to think I've got another 30 years in me so I want to only be involved in making a positive difference. I want to help the youth rather than kick drug dealers front doors down with my 'key' (size 12 feet) because of my own personal greed. At the time my thoughts were 'oh they're only scumbag drug dealers they deserve it' but I couldn't see through my own narcissistic thoughts.

Back then everything was about me. I know many of you reading this will think, Cockerill's full of shit and a leopard can't change his spots but I truly have. I'm here at the grand old age of 55, more or less an old man. I should have been murdered dozens of times over but I'm still here so I'm here to let you all know that a healthy body gives you a healthy mind. Don't follow me in what I did with the fighting and taxing but follow Brian Cockerill in the training side because I blew my chance and it still hurts today.

I'm telling everyone of you now who is reading this personally to get out there now and go for a jog! If you can't manage that then start by using the stairs in your homes. Training is everything to a healthy mind. I mean, how often do you see a miserable athlete? You just don't do you?!

Another thing I feel strongly to tell you all is PLEASE! PLEASE! PLEASE! don't start the drugs like I did.

One go spirals. One day your pissing about just with a bit of blow then the next you're a fully blown crackhead like I was and your life is fucking smashed to smithereens. Every bit of misery I've had in my life has been brought on by the misuse of drugs. I've lost good friends and family members and it gets to a point where you don't even go to people's funeral's. I got to a point where I was just sitting in an empty bedroom taking drugs being miserable and being psychotic so please listen to Uncle Brian and keep away from drugs.

Get yourself bang into school or college and if you're good at sport throw yourself into that. Keep away from the street fighting and if anybody tries to drag you into it just laugh and walk off, believe me you'll be more of a man. I wish you would all please keep away from the gangs and leave the knives alone. There's better things in life than having the police at your door, believe that from somebody who knows first-hand. Forget trying to be a gangster it's all utter bullshit. If you think it's clever to do what I did I'll tell you for free that its fucking not and I'm deeply ashamed.

Let me tell you now, I've been shot at, stabbed, hit with bars, ran over and had gangs jump me with weapons, etc, etc… I've had a life of none stop fighting and looking over my shoulder 24/7 and the armed response hunting me down regularly. In actual truth I've been arrested by the armed response/SAS 22 times which is a record for one man.

One of the chief of police congratulated me in a sarcastic manner and told me I'd broken the record for one man to have been arrested by the SAS the most! They just didn't send your average PC in numbers to bring Brian Cockerill in. The police knew I was clever and they'd send the best intellectual men in the force to break me and I'd just toy with them. Even some of the old retired officers have told me that when they'd retired. I used to tell the force I'd answer their questions to the best of my ability, I could be like all the others who say, "NO REPLY" but when I speak with them I always use perfect English and I'm always extremely polite. I tell them I'm not trying to be obtuse but my brains are expatiate, to put it bluntly I fucking do their heads in in a very civil way.

I've had a life where I get the blame for every murder in Teesside or if there was a shooting in Middlesbrough then instantly they'd come for me. I've never shot anyone but even when it's not me, 90% of the shootings in Teesside are done by people using my name and I've never even met them. Until 2019 I'd never used Facebook in my life but already there are seven different accounts with my name and picture.

I've lost count of people coming up to me saying, "ooh you ignorant bastard Bri I messaged you the other night and you just blanked me" and I'm like, "what you on about love I don't even use social media" but it was others pretending to be me for some strange bizarre reason. It's a funny old world out there isn't it! I suppose it's like when Jesse James and Billy the Kid were about and they were doing every robbery, well in Cleveland police's eyes even if it wasn't me pulling the trigger they were convinced that it was under my orders.

I think they had me down as being a baddie like Baron Greenback in Danger mouse and I was plotting evil everywhere I went which was never the case.

I've been questioned for a murder in Luton and God knows why they thought that one could even been me! In Cleveland police's eyes I was their Al Capone and even now that I'm trying to do good they hate it and I'm sure that several of my Facebook pages have been closed down by people in authority. Mind you, Al Capone was the first person to set up the soup kitchens in Chicago and I believe that's why they went for him over the tax because they needed to put him in his place and they couldn't get him for anything criminal. Even though Al Capone did what he did to mask his bad shit it was still good wasn't it?

You can't pretend to be a crackhead, you can't pretend to be a taxman, you either are one or you aren't one and my stories are there and have been seen by people.

I'm no Jackanory! There's people out there who've seen me involved in fights and at the time I thought it was big and cool, but in reality I was a fucking fool. Instead I should have been going for the world's strongest man. I want these kids to realise that the average binman makes more money over the year than being a criminal ever will. If you're an active criminal you'll only get away with it for so long then you go to fucking horrible stinking jail. When you're in prison you may think it's all cool but if you've got kids its them who are missing out on seeing their old man.

Back in 1990 the population of Teesside was 149,000 and today its 376,000 and I'd say more than half of that figure know the name of Brian Cockerill. Listen it's not for me to blow my own trumpet and as I've told you to be honest I'm fucking embarrassed about 75% of it, but I suppose the reason that people are fascinated with me is because I was a bareknuckle fighter who was out fighting the bad guys on a daily basis.

I NEVER used guns and I never ever hurt any normal average joe's who were just law-abiding citizens. I've always said if you lived in my world then you couldn't go to the police but if you were just a normal guy who worked for British Steel or in Lidl and you were getting bullied then of course you can go to the police. If you work and pay your taxes then that's your entitlement.

I never ever held it against anyone who ever rang the police if you were a decent person from the normal world but it's when people from my world who are gangsters who've fought me and when they've lost they've called the police and said, "Brian Cockerill's just beaten me up for nothing", even though it was a 50/50 fight and fully engaged by both parties then that's what gets me annoyed.

When I had a fight with a British heavyweight boxer and beat him up i.e. broke his jaw, etc, he made a statement to the police about me. You just can't be in both lanes, you're either a criminal or a straight goer. When I was beaten by a dozen or so men in Tommy Harrison's house (which I covered in my first book) I was kicked the shit out of. I had life-threatening injuries but did I fuck go to the police! In fact, when they were all arrested because their cars were clocked in the Ormesby area I even went to court and got them all off. If I was stabbed or shot and I had ten seconds to live and they said who done it I'd say, "Tatankum the Indian and Tommy Smith together." I chose that life and you have to stick that way in my opinion.

I've had several police officers begging me to make statements against people and my car crime would go missing as I've already told you earlier but I told them all to fuck off. I've always said, you can tell who the grasses are when they get the light prison sentences. Now I got thirty months for a dangerous driving offence when people were killing people and getting suspended sentences. It speaks volumes doesn't it?!

When I was doing debt collecting with Terry Dicko there was an Asian fella who hired us but made up a pack of lies to get someone innocent in trouble. Our view was, you can't call the dogs out for nothing like when you go hunting. I told this guy that me and Terry have had to get out of bed and he was just taking the piss making lies up on wanting someone to get a good hiding. I think he even tried to offer me £50 when it had probably cost me that in petrol money for the day. In the end he was made to pay and he'll think twice about being malicious again.

A lot of the time with me, when people see me they think, he'll be this big dopey cunt but I'm far from it. My brains expediential. People think I'll be your usual apoplectic (can't talk through anger) but I'm the opposite. The former manager of Manchester United Sir Alex Ferguson is the prime example of an apoplectic when you can't get the words out in time because you're so angry.

I think the only time I ever get raging in life is when I see a blatant liberty being taken for example someone being bullied and I just can't have that and will react. The one thing I've found over the years when they met me is people suddenly become hardcases. An old ex of mine used to do it all the time. I used to say to her, that's not clever. I don't know why but when people come into my company they want to tell me tales of how many fights they've had but really Brian Cockerill isn't about that.

If you see me come and talk to me about sport, Manchester United or helping charities my ears will prick up like an Alsatian. The overall message I want to get across is that I'm approachable to everyone.

In the last year of Paul Sykes' life the youth of Wakefield ridiculed him, he would say to them as he was bin picking, "better a has-been than a never was-been." I'm not a has-been because I can still fight for fun and I promise you that you still won't find a stronger man on the street than Brian Cockerill but I just chose for my life not to be like it was anymore.

I haven't found God, had a bang to the head or become mentally ill, but I just want to do good from now on and that's all. When I'm 80 years old I'm still going to be the former Taxman AKA The Boro Genghis Khan and that's probably going to stay with me to my grave. I think I'm looked at like this iconic image like your Lee Duffy's, Dave Garsides, The Sayers and many others. One man with a name who I won't mention said to me only recently, "Brian Cockerill beats the unbeatable." And when I asked him what he meant he said, "Duffy was unbeatable but you beat him. You went to fight Ernie Bewick but ended up shaking hands, Peter Hoe didn't wanna know, Viv Graham didn't wanna know, Paul Sykes didn't wanna know, you fought Ester from Guisborough and destroyed him, you fought the best fighter in Bishop Auckland who was nicknamed, 'The Dentist' because he was well known for hitting people with his big right hand and knocking all their teeth out and they ended up going to the dentist. The dentist came to Spennymoor and you hit him twice and broke his jaw then his brother got put out cold straight after."

This guy was reeling off all these things I'd done over the years and I was shocked he knew so much of what I'd been up to. He even knew about the time I fought two brothers from Spennymoor outside The Top Hat nightclub named Ellis who were boxers. I hit the first with my speciality which was a short right uppercut which had a delayed reaction then he fell. That was when his brother, who was also a name in the town, was a boxer and he screamed at me, "THAT'S MY FUCKING BROTHER" so straight away I've banged him and said, "you can fucking join him asleep then." I left them both asleep side by side.

If you don't know Spennymoor it's a rough little town in County Durham and what I did there was like someone coming into Middlesbrough and knocking Brian Cockerill and Lee Duffy out sparko within seconds. There's no doubt I made a reputation but it's going to take me for the rest of my life to lose it. In my fighting days there was less cameras and nobody had mobile camera phones so you could get away with all sorts. These days if you've got bad intentions and are some kind of doorman or figure in authority you'll be found out and your mask will slip. Today I would rather be loved for being a nice man.

Now I'm not slagging my friend in this book but my buddy Lee Duffy used to say to me, "Brian I can walk into a pub in one minute and empty it" but my aim was to fill it in a minute. I remember going to The Mile House in Roseworth once and around 40-50 Asian taxi drivers turned up that night alone just to meet me because people love me.

I'm not daft though I know a bit of it's to do with the curiosity of the alleged caveman Brian Cockerill. Another night I went in a pub called The Gables near Coulby Newham with Lee Benzley and it was absolutely rammed but there wasn't one fight that night when it had been having a lot of trouble around that time.

At the end of the night the manager came up to me and gave me a bottle of Moet & Chandon and told me he'd took more money tonight than ever because everybody came to see me, this wasn't long after I did my first book with Steve Richards. When Mark and Bernie Owens went and got married. I actually gave Bernie away that day but there was more pics taken of me than the bride & groom.

"I walked in and about 12 lads smashed me over the head with a hammer, stabbed me in the back and put a gun to my head. I dropped a few of them and threw them about the house."

"I was about 24 stone at the time so they couldn't put me down. It went on for about 10 minutes. I was stabbed and had 176 stiches and lost three pints of blood."

"They battered me with baseball bats and hammers and stabbed me. They left me for dead and said, 'That will be the end of him.' I went to hospital and they said if I was not so big I would probably be dead."

Brian Cockerill on the horrors that happened inside Tommy Harrison's house back in 1992.

CHAPTER 21

WHAT IF'S EH???

Today I sit here at 55 years old full of regrets. I'm mad at myself because I should have been the world's strongest man. I'm annoyed at myself because I allowed myself to be manipulated by others into doing their dirty work and I can't turn back the clock. Every time I've went to have a fight with someone and sort problems out it's never been for myself. I've never burgled a house in my life, saying that I've kicked a few doors in. I've never shoplifted in my life but I've been arrested for every crime under the sun but I've only been sent down for driving offences.

I'm not trying to blow my own trumpet here but if I went into the world's strongest man, there were men beforehand such as Mark & Ali Johnson, Pecca, Snax, Peter Ayton, Terry Cooper, Rob Cook and even Eddy Ellwoods' mate Denny Hoyle. Denny said I was the biggest thing he's ever seen in his life and so did Terry Stockell. Kevin Kilty was blown away by me at times and was there when I did the 2000lbs leg press as well as Mark and Paul Debrick (God rest him). I do have the footage of me bending the Olympic bar which I'll use for my documentary with the same names that are in this book. It does bother me these days that people know the name Brian Cockerill in the same bracket as Lee Duffy as some bareknuckle streetfighter but in the harsh reality what hurts me was what I should and could have been. The thing I'm thankful for is that I'm still here, it's too late for my mate Lee Duffy but I'd imagine he'd be alongside me doing what I'm doing now with his bullet holes.

It's not only me by the way its Stephen Sayers who's well and truly turned his life around and is now making films and so on. Today I want to speak in just a positive light because these kids idolise me. I never backed down from a fight and I'll never back down from helping someone.

Quite often I get embarrassed because I get asked for my picture taken but I don't feel I'm an anybody for people to ask such a thing of me. Another thing that bugs me is I should have been a multi-millionaire now. The lads who I used to give money to or give them hordes of E's weren't daft because they kept their money and I blew it. If you ask me what my biggest regret is today I'd have to say taking drugs and especially going on the crack! People might be reading this thinking, aren't you ashamed of the fights you had? Well, truthfully my answer to that is my fights were 50/50 with other big guys. I didn't walk up and punch people for nothing because that's what The Duffer did!

Sometimes I'd pull Lee aside and say, "what you fucking doing man?" Peter Hoe was totally different to Lee Duffy altogether in that aspect but that kid could have a fight as well. Peter Hoe was over 6ft and maybe 15-16st but his hand speed and boxing skills were phenomenal, he could have been a professional fighter any day of the week no problem at all. His little brother Anthony was even better he beat good solid pro's like Paul Hodkinson, Billy Hardy and even Eddie Ellwood.

The tragedy that the Hoe family have went through losing Peter, Tommy and Robbie is truly heart breaking. There's only Brian and Anthony out of the brothers left. What really fucking turns my stomach is the way them two dirty bastards (David and Terry Reed) both tried to befriend me in jail but I fucking chased the pair and they ran like fuck, the pair of cowardly rats. Just before Peter's death they'd both been to fight him and Peter was a really lovely man.

I was a bad man taxing scum of the earth drug dealers, but my thinking then was that if I didn't do that as a vocation then I wouldn't have been able to treat my family to the luxuries I've given them. I know today that the street kids look up to me but I don't want them to look up to me for being the taxman, if you have to look up to me then please do it for the training I've dedicated my life to. Follow me by helping people.

If there's one message more than any that I want to get across in this book is that any of you can change your life at any age or any day of the week. Forget saying, "I'm going to do it after Christmas" but Christmas never ever comes. When you start training it creates natural endorphins which is magnificent for the human mind. Don't think you're going to become Mr Universe right away. At the start you might only lift tins of beans in Asda bags going up and down slowly but the bonus is its already started. Don't look at Brian Cockerill or Lee and think you want to be exactly like us. You just need to be the best you that you can be and everything will fall into place.

If you wanted to put on weight and were 10st and you've gotten to 12st you've bettered yourself. If you want to lose weight and you're 22st and you've got down to 21st you've bettered yourself trust me on this, I have a degree in diets and discipline. I keep telling you I'm 55 years old but if I could sit and give the 19 – 26 year olds in gangs any advice at all then it would be keep the fuck away from drugs, listen to policemen, schoolteachers and probation officers because they're not the enemy, they are there to help.

I know this sounds terrible but if anybody of any figure of authority came up and tried to talk to me when I was young I'd think, shut up you stupid old bastard! When I was a teenager I'd think, what do I want to listen to you for you're thirty odd years old!!!

As I've said for the past six months since me and Jamie Boyle teamed up I'd love to go around the schools and deliver the anti-knife crime talks because if doesn't matter how small someone is it only takes the strength to pull the trigger to kill someone the size of Brian Cockerill. It could be that I had a life worse than Viv Graham, Lee Duffy and Speedy Hornsby so why the fuck is Brian Cockerill alive and still walking the streets?! If underworld crime was a business I was Bill Gates, Steve Jobs or Simon Cowell, but I know that's not something to be proud of.

I'd like to think the only good thing is god spared me because I'm a good person, and that he has found a job for me to do.

Now I'm 55 and I'd like to say I've finally seen the light and after this I'm not going to be given anymore second chances and nor do I deserve any. I've had bareknuckle fights, I've ran in houses knowing that people are armed with all kinds of evil instruments.

Donal Macintyre once asked me if I was scared, but I told him I wasn't fucking bothered. Amanda used to say I could turn it on and off like a tap. Amanda said that's what happened to that Nintendo guy that night, she saw it coming long before I blitzed him, but he was a scumbag bully anyway who deserved it.

Today in 2020 I can still turn it on and off but it takes longer. If I ever flew into a rage it would have to be if somebody hurt my brother Bobby, Emma or my friend Jamie Boyle.

Going back to the clairvoyant, Gary Fowler, he said, "one day Brian you're going to have the most power in the whole of Teesside." You know something? That's where I got the idea of becoming the mayor from, even though I never ended up running for mayor in the end, I did remarkably well campaigning, but I ruined it with the drugs. It would have been interesting reading wouldn't it if I'd actually went and gone for it but you never know what the future holds. That isn't over as far as I'm concerned so only time will tell.

I'll never forget being laid there in my drug induced state and Gary telling me the reason that I was still alive was because God had a plan for me but to be honest I wasn't listening to him. I thought it was just a load of bullshit but God forgave me and please forgive me Gary but I'm now a believer.

Even as little as two years ago I saw Gary Fowler and he was still at it, "God's got a purpose for you Brian very soon but you still don't realise it yet." Now I believe god sent me that little weirdo Jamie Boyle so he could give me the platform I needed to reach the tens of thousands as I'm now doing. Although I refuse to give that Jamie Boyle any credit, its Mrs B, aka Shirley Whirley who is the real star.

"Stop trying to control everything and just let go!

LET GO!

CHAPTER 22

THE ART OF VIOLENCE

The truth was Sykesy was a total gobshite in the end when he was drunk.

Up until around 1991 Paul Sykes was as dangerous and as powerful as you get for fighting men. Maybe it was karma or just his fate but he ended up a tramp being beaten daily by the youth of Wakefield. Most days the kids would crack eggs on Sykesy's head and he couldn't do a thing about it because he was that drunk, weak and vulnerable.

I know Sky Sports presenter and former world cruiser weight champion Johnny Nelson told Jamie Boyle in one of his books, "the thing is those kids who terrorised Paul once over in his final days would not have any idea that once upon a time the fear that man could instil into the hardest of men." Even Peter Fury (Tyson's trainer and uncle) said, "you wouldn't even look at that man sideways he was a dangerous, dangerous man."

Another name I was linked with was the total unit Viv Graham who I met in Durham prison in 1989, I was only in one week. I didn't know Viv a great deal but when I spent the time in that week with him he was squatting 4/5 plates and I was doing 8. When he was benching 5 plates I was benching 6 so I was a lot stronger than him.

In reality Viv was one huge man, around 20st and just under 6ft. To be honest I didn't really have much to do with Viv and in truth the only things we ever said to each other was small talk, that was until a few years later I made friends with them bad boys, The Sayers. Most weekends I would be out raving with Stephen and Michael and they'd come to stay at my house along with Stevie Abingdon and Manny Burgo Jnr, Manny beat Viv Graham also in an amateur boxing ring.

They were all brilliant lads who could seriously have a fight for fun. It was around that time I really got to know Sunderland's 'Rocky Marciano' Ernie Bewick and boy did he put himself out for me, it was unbelievable.

I got to know the world champion cage fighter Ian Freeman who is another great guy along with Kev Rich and Terry Rich and not forgetting Hartlepool's Richy Horsley who I love and have so much respect for.

I suppose how I came about almost fighting with Viv Graham was at a rave in Stockton and I had a fight with a lad named Gilly, truth be known I just slapped him with the palm of my hand and his face split wide open and his jaw was totally bust. I only did that because Gilly was hitting a man named Raymond (Basil) Mann from Grove Hill, Kevin Kilty was there and watched the whole episode. I do have to say I felt sick after I saw the state of his face after I slapped him because he looked like The Joker from Batman it was horrific and didn't make me feel too clever at all, but at that time I was almost touching 24st.

Afterwards the story Gilly told people was Brian Cockerill and six lads jumped him to put him in such a state but a few of the door lads like Addish, Mark Debrick and Mark Johnson were there so they knew it was utter bullshit. Yes it was a bad thing to happen but he was the one being sadistic and bullying the weaker man in Basil Mann. What happened from there was that I was told Gilly's dad had a scrapyard with a lot of money and it was him who offered Viv Graham to come and bash me.

I know for a fact that he paid Viv Graham £10,000 for him to do me in because it was Armstrong who told me the full thing. It was actually funny how I got it out of Armstrong because although he used to talk to me, he only knew me as Big Bri! So when he asked me if I knew Brian Cockerill I asked him why? That was when he confirmed to me that Gilly's dad had just put together £10,000 to have me done in by Viv graham.

When I told him, "I'm Brian Cockerill you doughnut" he couldn't believe it! I know that as time went on people were throwing more money at Viv to do me in and Viv's answer was, "nor I don't really wanna fight Bri" but as time escalated and them naughty boys, The Sayers got involved, Stephen and Michael wanted me to fight him with them both putting in £25,000 each as well as Jimmy and Gary Robb who had The Blue Monkey rave and were literally millionaires then got involved and that's how it became this £50,000 fight which was supposed to take place at the Quayside or in Sunderland football ground but that was knocked back.

Anyway I go up one day to Tyneside with my girlfriend in our tiny little Escort, this must have been around 1992 the year after we lost the Duffer and I thought I'd do him proud and hunt Viv Graham down for the craic like he used to and she dropped me at a nightclub in Newcastle which was called The Madison. I had a tracksuit on as I usually do. It's not that I don't own any smart clothes because I have £500 suits, it's just I'm that big and anything apart from tracksuits and t-shirts aren't comfortable. To cut a long story short I walked into the nightclub in just a shell suit looking like M.C Hammer and a pair of army boots. The reason Lee Duffy was always in trainers and shorts was that he was ready to fight.

Anyway, I was told I wouldn't be allowed in the club but as soon as I was told that, another Geordie bouncer barged over and told him in a stage whisper, "DO YOU WANT TO FUCKING DIE AND HAVE US ALL KILLED? THAT'S BRIAN COCKERILL YA MAD CUNT!" Well the truth is that these were all Viv Graham's doormen and this was a Friday night and he'd usually be in every Friday night without fail.

One Geordie who didn't even know who I was, said to me, "if Viv comes in and sees you like that then he'll probably start on you" and I just thought, will he now? So, I sat there drinking on my own all night until it was closing time but he never turned up.

Now I can't tell you he was tipped off that Big Bri was up from Teesside dressed like an American rapper because I've got no proof, but Stephen and Michael Sayers told me that because apparently he was there weekly on a Friday. The funny thing at that time in Newcastle was that after the nightclubs shut at 2am it was game over.

It wasn't like in Middlesbrough where you have several Blues clubs and believe me everything happened in them places, think of the pub in Star Wars and you're halfway there, in fact people would probably be swinging Lightsabre's around and nobody would bat an eyelid. The Blues was the jungle and Lee Duffy was the Lion of that jungle before he got killed because I didn't bother with that as much because I was training all the time.

One man's name who'd I'd like to mention in this book is Ernie Bewick. Now although Ernie and myself have never fought, I'd like to thank him because he was like an older brother to me. Sunderland's Ernie used to teach me things which brought me on wisely. Ernie's favourite hero was Rocky Marciano and not many people know this but him and Viv Graham actually fought in the amateurs with Ernie beating him handily. You wouldn't think in a million years by just looking at Ernie that he could fight like he could.

There was another big fighter from Newcastle named Billy Robinson who's a good 6ft 4 and 20st plus, well Billy smacked Ernie on the sneak but Ernie still beat him. Although Ernie beat Viv Graham in the boxing ring they were supposed to fight on the cobbles but Viv copped that one as well.

Going back to myself I've fought and beat Brian Sterlo the best fighter in Billingham and I destroyed all 6ft 3 of him within seconds. I've also been threatened by the big names whether they were real or made up, names such as The Richardson's from London (but in the end I became good friends with young Charlie Richardson). I'll never forget being in a pub down London and I was dancing away in this green shirt, at the time I was around 23st but because I was so ripped I must have looked easy 26st and when I dance I tend to shadow box so it was old Charlie Richardson (now sadly passed) that came over to me and said, "please calm it down big fella because everybody's on edge in here" but I was only having a good time and just being boisterous. All the doormen were stood reading newspapers in a pitch-black nightclub pretending not to see me.

Another villain I was going to be paid to fight was John Palmer who'd been part of the gold bullion robbery in 1983 which I was supposed to be part of but I was replaced by a man named Andy Winder who went abroad in my place and got shot so if that's not proof that God's not looking out for me I don't know what is.

One of my biggest regrets though was never meeting "Pretty Boy" Roy Shaw because he sent me some lovely messages and I was part of Bernard O'Mahoney's Faces book, he used to get dead excited at the thought of meeting me but sadly we never met and that's a big regret of mine. Jamie Boyle went on to write a fantastic book called Mean Machine which is about Roy Shaw, with his only son Gary and I believe at the moment they're working on their second book and a documentary.

The Noonan family were another family always asking Donal Macintyre for my number but I was never really into that game whereas they were. It's a sad mentality but someone from that world once said, "Brian people are fascinated with you because of what you've been about" and yes I can get it. I mean when I was in Liverpool prison there was 1700 lags and over 600 screws but I was seen as the daddy.

If you want me to name the prisons off hand I've been in they are Holme House, Durham, Walton, Acklington, Cumbria, Thorp Arch and Whealston because I was so volatile. I'll never forget this lovely big screw came to my door when I was ready to go to war with about twelve of them. As I was waving them in one by one, one of them slightly paused and said, "please big fella can I have a word?" I was still full of rage but as he talking it was sinking in that it was total sense what he was saying to me.

He said it was inevitable that I'd break 3-4 jaws before I was overpowered and then I'd spend my life down the block like Charlie Bronson or Paul Sykes. That screw did me a massive favour and I even shook his hand because I was just so thankful for his thought provoking words because I was ready to do treble life sentences and the rest. I was a fucking raging bull. I was in jail for a white-collar crime such as driving and bunked up with murderers and armed robbers.

I can't finish this book without mentioning my brothers Jamie, Bobby and sister Catherine and my nieces Jamie-Lee and Katie. Not forgetting my brother Peter who passed away.

Listen, you've all read my book by now so you know I'm not exactly a full shilling myself but if I can help you lot in any way just know that I'll be there, please believe me seriously. I can't come and help you though if you're fighting with that neighbour down the road and you need someone bashing because I'm well out of that game.

Another thing I'd like to point out is I don't get involved with domestics so if you've made your bed with her/him you better lay in it.

God forgive me for saying this and please believe me I'm not trying to sound big headed but I have a huge following out there, as in hardcore fans, I'd like to thank you from the bottom of my heart for giving me a second chance and giving me the attention in reading this or watching The Resurrection of Brian Cockerill documentary because that's shown you all, the tens of thousands that read the Steve Richards book and watched the Donal Macintyre documentary that that wasn't the real Brian Cockerill it was made up for dramatised television.

I think the biggest thank you I'd like to give is to that little weirdo Jamie Boyle and his gorgeous wife Mrs Shirley Whirley. It was Jamie who came and sniffed me out like a Bloodhound when I was in a bad place at a horrendous time when he wasn't even sure I might have brayed him for what he typed up in The Terry Dicko 1 – Laughter, Madness and Mayhem book (total utter weirdo or balls of steel I'll let you work that one out with Jamie Boyle) because even though he didn't say it, he typed up what Terry Dicko told him in the end.

Truth being told I wasn't a fan of Jamie Boyle's when I used use to watch him on YouTube or see him in the papers. He had some balls coming looking for me in the first place though but the blokes transformed my life and he's turned out to be one of the most genuine best people I've ever met. I know me and the strange little fucker are going to do lots of things i.e. documentaries, books, etc, etc…. The pair of us have only just begun our fight to straighten Teesside out. Jamie and Shirley-Anne Boyle will be my friends for life and anything they ever need I'll be there.

Jamie asked me once, he said, "was I drugged in jail like Sykes and Bronson because I was that much of a handful?" Ha'way Jamie I don't sleep, I'm like a robot. I maybe have six hours a day when I'm plugged in and all of a sudden when I was in certain prisons I just couldn't get out of my bed, so I think that answers your question sunshine!

Usually I've had people say I'm just hyperactive but since I've got older I've got a racing brain and it makes me go around in circles. Even when I was in bad bouts of depression my mind would be constantly telling me, I'll fucking snap your neck if I get within arm's length of you blah blah. This may come as a shock but I'm not a violent man, I just hate bullies and bad manners and if God spares me and I'm here in thirty years my mannerisms will be the same.

I'd like to thank my mother Mary and dad Jimmy Cockerill for bringing me up. Going back to little Terry Dicko, Terry's my pal even though he slagged me off to bits in his first book. If you want my opinion on why he did that then it was because I was his rock for 26 years and then I left him (we fell out over a woman). I missed him and I know he missed me so we've now kissed and made up. I'd never hurt Terry no matter what he's said about me in the past. I know Terry's said a lot of hurtful things about me but at the time he was going through a bad time with his Mrs, daughter and Cleveland police so we'll just let sleeping dogs lie. Beyond that Terry Dicko has been a loyal friend to me so he's done far better for me than just have his little rant in his book. I could have done the same in this book but I chose to let it go over my head and be a grown up.

"A favour can get you killed faster than a bullet."

Emma Cockerill

CHAPTER 23

BAD DAYS AT THE OFFICE

Although taxing is the most dangerous job in the world it does bring its funny moments. Like the time I walked into a house of drug dealers and lined about 17 of them up, only when they all emptied their pockets all they had between them was one ecstasy tablet and a £5 note. Another time I went into a well-known crack house on Princess Road. Once I was inside I assessed the situation, you have to don't you because its life and death. Anyway I clocked a room full of yardies and in my mind I was already plotting to do the lot.

Everyone in them crack houses knew who I was and they were fully aware what I'm about. I'm a drug dealers nightmare, I'm Satan, I'm Beelzebub, I'm the one and only anti-Christ and if you see me knock on your crack house door you better get on your knees and say your Hail Mary's because believe me evil in the shape of a 20st plus man has risen from Hell and is coming for you and all your ill-gotten gains purely down for my own greed. Back then that was the reality.

Going back to me analysing the situation, I was thinking, I can crack him with a right hand then come back onto the other with a left hook, then put his head through the telly but what I didn't realise was there were two girls sat on the settee with a blanket over them. I badly underestimated them as underneath that blanket they had knives, hammers and CS gas with my name on them.

When I was looking around the front room I saw one of the African men holding a screwdriver so that's when I thought, I'm going to tax these cunts big time! To cut a long story short I was getting more irritated so I shouted, "ALL YOU CUNTS IN ERE ARE GETTING TAXED NOW" So in any situation like that, and believe me I've only been in a few I start flinging bodies about and punching peoples lights out, when all of a sudden these two extremely large women have lifted the blanket and CS gassed me straight in the boat race and honest to god I was like, "AAAAAAAARRRGHHH" and I thought I was really fucking dying and couldn't see a thing but at the same time I was still fighting away with this full house of crack dealers.

In the end I picked one of the big fat bastard ladies up and used her as a human shield to get to the front door. My thinking was if one of them was going to hit me they were going to clobber this fat cow first. One of my vivid memories was when I was leaving the crack house one of the dealers came and flung a knife but it just missed me and stuck in the side of the door, thank god. I got outside and I got into my car and luckily there was a bottle of water in my car so I poured it into my eyes but they were still on fire.

Anyway after around 5-7 minutes I get my eyesight back but by then the full shift of Middlesbrough police had pulled up as well as my usual mates the armed response and told me to piss off and basically do one, they knew what Big Bri was up to again.

In fact even though this gang had thousands of pounds worth of crack cocaine it was the police who gave them a private escort back to the A19. I'm not going to lie I was like a Honey badger waiting to rob some honey, I was prepared to do everyone in that house for the money and all the crack but I didn't think for one moment that the two fat birds were as deadly as they turned out to be.

Another funny time I was taxing with Lee Duffy on Hartington Road in Stockton. Well as I've told you Lee Duffy had a bit of a sadistic sense of humour and as he was taxing the black African guy, he asked him, "who's the best fighter out of me and him?" pointing at me, then himself. The black lad who had dreadlocks like The Predator looked at me, then looked at Lee, then looked at me then looked at Lee and just took a run and jumped through the window like the priest in The Exorcist. I just looked at Lee and said, "he deserves to get away for that!"

Lee of course couldn't help but nick his telly because he couldn't help thieving anything he could find and when we got downstairs he said to Neil Booth who was waiting in the car, "did you see that man who's just done a runner through the window?" I'll never forget Neil Booth's expression, he replied, "did I see him? He almost landed on me." But that's just how much fear Duffy had over people. If you saw that man jumping through a window in a movie you'd think, that's impossible! Obviously the fear of Brian Cockerill and Lee Duffy was too much and he risked his life. To Lee everything was funny even battering people, he just never took nothing or nobody seriously.

You're reading this book now many decades on and you think that there's so many serious points but I've been involved with some utterly bonkers shit as well.

Like the time the bodybuilder Lee Little lost his job. I rang his boss and I said, "Lee won't be coming in today because me and him are going to be taking ecstasy together all day." The poor bastard got the sack because of me but I rang his boss up and told him I was Brian Cockerill so he better give Lee his job back or else. I would often go raving with Lee Little at a place called The Powerhouse which used to be on Redcar Sea Front.

Anyway me and Lee used to go back to a guy's flat named Mally on Queens Street, Redcar to recuperate whilst we got ready to go back out raving. I was laid completely flat out on Mally's sofa when I hear a load of loud voices from a gang of rowdy lads. As soon as Mally and Lee hear the voices they go outside to see what the confrontations are about and they say it's all the hardcases from a nearby pub named The Hydro which was a hangout for the Boro F.C Redcar casuals. Well they must have been around a dozen or so of these hardnuts from The Hydro and basically they'd all come around to Mally's flat to have a go at Mally and Lee so now there's this really baying angry crowd on the front of Mally's flat that are all baying for blood.

It's funny because Lee Little comes out at the front of the house and he sees this angry group of vigilantes running away and he starts thinking he's Dickie Rock, he then realises there's this fucking big shadow coming from behind and its only then that he realises the Hydro mob weren't running from Lee Little they were running from Brian Cockerill.

I can laugh as much as I want but the facts are I have been arrested for seven murders, seven shootings and I've had seven powder residue tests which have all come back negative. I must have been arrested for 20 -25 section 18's but never been charged with one. I've been responsible for around 18 guardsman fractures but that was in a life that has long since died. I kicked four police doors off for fun and years later they put cages inside which always made me think, did they do that for me?

When I worked as a bouncer in Henry Africa's in Stockton and we had all types of acts on such as Shawaddywaddy, Mudd, Four Tops and even Bernard Manning (he would go on to take a shine to me whenever he was playing). Every time he would see me he would say, "before we do anything tonight I want that big bastard (pointing at me) with the big shoulders. I asked, "me Mr Manning?" He replied, "call me Bernard and yes because there's nobody getting past you is there?" On this night it was a Monday but Bernard was a knockout and he told everyone that "if I say its Wednesday night its fucking Wednesday night." Bernard was a very funny man close up and he's sadly missed.

"Out of sight, out of mind."

Proverb

CHAPTER 25

A HAPPY ENDING AND AN ANGEL SENT

This maybe the last chapter of this book and it's probably the corniest, cheesiest one because I truly believe I was sent an angel from above by the lord putting Emma Nixon back in my life. I first met little Emma when I was living and training in Redcar with Frankie Atherton and I bumped into this blonde bombshell who was around 16 but totally stunning. After we got to know each other we started going on the beach and even a few dates but around 1990/91 my mind was on other things doing shit with Darth Vader AKA Lee Duffy.

Also very shamefully of me for a start was I was mad on the drugs, partying and taking E's for fun so me and Emma drifted apart and that was all caused by me being a dickhead and I broke her heart. It was such a shame that I hurt Emma that way because her mam died of cancer when she was only 15 and since then she had to more or less fend for herself from such a young age.

The poor girls had a hard life. Emma isn't proud of it but she defended herself in any way she could and that even led to her selling narcotics and messing about with dodgy credit cards for Eston's Paul Bryan. Emma was a mess with anxiety and struggled to leave the house unless it was to scrape a bit of dodgy dealing together which is really no life for a girl of her young age.

When I went to jail we split up and when I eventually regained my freedom I went to look for her but I was told that she had died of an overdose. Truth be told it was her friend who had died of an overdose but I didn't know any different. This time it was my heart that was broken and I thought Emma was my one and I'd lost her and she'd well and truly slipped through the net.

You know the funny thing is it was Jamie and Shirley Boyle who told me to go on Facebook and connect with some old friends because up until then I thought it was all evil. It was on the 21st of November 2019 that I received a message from this Emma Nixon saying, "Hiya Bri are you ok?" Straight away I thought it can't be my old Emma because she's dead, it's somebody taking the fucking piss here! By then I'd got really paranoid so I asked her if she was really Emma Nixon where did she meet me? Her reply was, near Leo's Nightclub on Redcar Sea Front.

I won't bore you with the in's and outs' of our first date other than my younger brother Bobby locked me out of our car so we couldn't visit Emma in Redcar as I'd promised her. Our poor Bobby always gets the blame in our family even if it wasn't him. When 9/11 happened I'm sure our Bobby was linked to that as well!

The funny thing is Emma came to mine then stayed for eight days and then we got matching tattoo's and haven't left each other's sides since. People have been saying, that's a bit of a whirlwind romance but I think me and Emma should have been together decades ago.

We already told each other we loved each other again on the internet before we met up so I believe it was truly fate. I must admit though, as much as I loved my Emma I did have to ask myself, "HANG ON A MINUTE! are you still a mad head?" because trust me that girl loved to party. Even by Emma's own admittance she was "crazy" but now she had settled down and currently works for the church which I was so happy to hear considering what I'm doing now.

It was just a coincidence of so many things (as well as me living like a prat) that I really couldn't see what was going on when we first split up. Emma's had no children, I've got no biological children, but she's got an American Bulldog and I've got an American Akita. Even though I've been a gangland enforcer, dick, prat, etc, etc… I believe it was destiny to have me and Emma together in the end. These days Emma tells me she can't believe that she got me back and that this time she's never going to let me go. Even though she's said all that she's severely warned me I'm not to be involved in any debt collecting with people where I end up going to jail and then she loses me and I end up like all the other idiots.

It was only the other night me and Emma went for a meal in Redcar when this guy was circling me and when he got me on his own he was offering me crackpipes. Emma's told me she won't have any bullshit or she'll leave me in the gutter and rightly so. I always wanted like a 1950s wife where they stay with you and get married to you for good and that's what Emma exactly is. As soon as we got engaged Emma wanted to get in touch with the church at Easterside with Tony Grange. Whatever happens my old life has well and truly died. If a pathetic old crackhead like me can change his life then I promise you now, that all of you reading this can.

If anyone sees me from now on please please, please don't be scared. Come up for a hug and tell me all about yourself and I'll be all ears like a dog. Please people believe me I'm not some monster. Come and give me a cuddle and I'll know you've read this book and then you'll know the real person folks and remember, "carrying knives destroys lives!"

The last word goes to my better half Emma:

"Brian's mine for life now and if anyone wants to use him for his dirty work then they'll have to go through me because he's the love of my life."

In truth Emma left and went to live in Liverpool for over a decade. The truth was Emma and I were split up well over a quarter of a century but Emma stayed madly in love with me and she said when we finally got back together it was almost like we had not been apart for more than a month. This might sound bizarre but we are both as happy as we've ever been. This might sound soppy but I truly believe that God sent me an angel in my Emma and we both married for the first time in early 2020. I'd like everybody to know that me and Emma are born again Christians and we're going to continue to do Gods work and I've even been Christened by Tony Grange in the sea like Jesus.

I am in a better place now than I've ever been before, which this time last year I never ever thought would be possible. Emma Cockerill is my drug now although she takes the mick out of me daily. Emma once had an American Bulldog which she called, "Monkey." Then she got this toy orangutan for the bedroom which she calls "Chimp" but she says the only reason she got me back was she wanted a Silverback Gorilla and named it "Brian".

My pastor at my church in Easterside (Tony Grange) has totally touched my spirit because I haven't even thought about drugs in almost a year. Trust me I'm done with that vile shite and from now on Big Bad Bri is only here to help people. If you're reading this then I want to tell you I love you! At one point in my life I was living so recklessly I didn't care if I was going to even make thirty. I used to think if I get killed I get killed so I'm going to enjoy myself as much as I can in the short time I'm here like Lee Duffy did. I definitely still didn't see me here at 55 years old. I used to say I couldn't take the thousands of money with me so I blew it on shite or gave it away whereas now I work hard for my money and I'm a different man, better late than never eh?!

If you all take one thing away from reading my book then just please, please, please never make same the mistakes that I did. I fucked everything up when I could have done more. I've hurt the ones I've loved. Yes I've done so much bad but I truly believe I'm not a bad person. Everybody deserves second chances no matter how old or washed up we are! If I have to spend the rest of my live repenting for my sins helping kids and supporting ant-knife campaigns then I'll happily do that with my new wife. Myself and my new wife my Emma are now only on one path well and truly and that's the one Jesus Christ has set out for us. If you can find it in your hearts to forgive me then thank you kindly. If you can't then I totally understand. At the end of the day we'll all be judged one day by the biggest God of them all.

Thank you all so much for giving me a second chance and reading my book.

God bless each and every one of you and remember to keep smiling and fighting every day. There's no shame in asking for help, no matter who you are!

Love Big Bri XX

Also available

The Sayers
Tried and Tested at the Highest Level

By Stuart Wheatman & Steve Wraith

Coming from a huge close-knit family of street traders long before it was legalised, Stephen Sayers spent his early years on the barrows, witnessing constant brushes with the law. Aunties and uncles were frequently incarcerated and a hatred and distrust of authority swelled within the younger members of the family. The scene was set. Standing alongside his brothers and cousins in vicious street fights and feuds with rival gangs, they've been linked to multi-million pound armed robberies, extortion, unsolved gangland murders and protection rackets. Those links made them a formidable force in the criminal underworld. Stephen gives us a first-hand account of growing up as a Sayers and living up to the reputation the name carries. He didn't just carve out a criminal career, he wrote it in blood on the streets. If you've heard the rumours... if you believe them... the Sayers run Newcastle.

ISBN: 978-1-9114820-5-5

Also available

Lee Duffy: The Whole of the Moon

by Jamie Boyle

ISBN: 978-1-9125430-7-6

A book which has taken over 25 years to arrive. The definitive story of the man who held an eight year reign of terror over the town of Middlesbrough. Containing many first-hand and previously unheard accounts from some of Duffy's closest friends and associates.

Lee Duffy 'The Whole of the Moon' Documentary DVD

From Media Arts

August 25th 1991 at 3.55am saw the inevitable end to Lee Duffy's life. Everyone knew Lee's existence on this planet would be brief, including Lee and his Mother but the news Teesside was waking up to that gloriously sunny morning would rock it to its foundations. Lee has been gone now more years than he was alive although he is still spoken of as if he was here yesterday. Lee Duffy was arguably Teesside's most prolific criminal but where did his violent side stem from? Was he a figure of evil or misunderstood?